...and stumbled on a morning

BILL AUSTIN

Tyndale House
Publishers, Inc.
Wheaton, Illinois

Library of Congress
Catalog Card Number
78-57964
ISBN 0-8423-0069-4,
cloth

First printing, March
1979.
Printed in the United
States of America.

TO MARGIE

One light

that never

dimmed

I came here
seeking light in darkness,
running from the dawn,
and stumbled on a morning.

—Maxwell Anderson
Winterset (Act III)

CONTENTS

TWO
Running from the Dawn

THREE
And Stumbled on a Morning

TWILIGHT

THE TELEPHONE I held in my hand had so often been an instrument of help, a bond for friendship, a bearer of good news. Now I stared at it as though it were a foreign object and a vicious enemy. I wished I had never picked it up.

I had called the doctor to help me get through the afternoon of public service and personal pain which lay ahead of me. As pastor of a local congregation, it was my responsibility to conduct the funeral service for a prominent physician, a member of our church, and a personal friend.

His death had been tragic and untimely, a heart attack in middle age, while he had teenage children still at home and years of service ahead of him. Yet, after pastoring for twenty-five years, I had grown familiar with the unfamiliar patterns of death, so I knew that the physical pain and dizziness I was experiencing were due to more than depression and tension.

I told the doctor that my symptoms were more intense than they had been since my problems had begun several weeks earlier. He told me how much to increase my medication and insisted that I come to see him again soon, implying that there was something more we should discuss.

Frustrated and impatient, I pressed him into discussing the many neurological tests I had had recently. As he hesitated, I sensed that he knew, or at least thought, something definite. Finally, when I would not relent, he conceded that he had concluded I had multiple sclerosis.

Emotional numbness spread through me like a protective anesthetic, and I somehow mechanically got to the church in time for the funeral. Practically the entire local medical community was there to pay tribute to their fallen colleague. I quickly spotted the worried-looking neurologist whose somber diagnosis was still echoing in my ears. My mind alternated between trying to comfort the bereaved family and friends, and wanting to cry out to all those doctors for help.

I spoke briefly on "Death, Be Not Proud," and I consciously wondered if the diagnosis I had received less than an hour ago was of a terminal illness. I knew so little about this disease, but I knew enough to feel terribly vulnerable, insecure, and afraid. I was forty-three years old; how many more years before someone would conduct a funeral service for me? Would they be years of pain and invalidism?

Where could I go for help? How could I minister to others when I needed ministering to so desperately myself?

The questions had started. The night had begun.

ONE

...seeking light in darkness...

When I looked for good,
then evil came unto me: And
when I waited for light,
there came darkness.

Job 30:26

RACING THE SUNSET

The light is short because of darkness (Job 17:12).

THE NIGHT seldom begins suddenly. On rare occasions darkness may come swiftly, with a winter storm or total eclipse of the sun. But usually it eases itself in gradually and quietly, hesitating slightly on the horizon, as though it might change its mind and let the day continue. Then, in a rush of finality it folds the light away with a smug gloating over momentary conquest.

The student reaches subconsciously to turn on the desk lamp. The housewife flips a nearby switch, continuing her supper preparations without interruption. The weary traveler fumbles for the correct knob on the instrument panel. A long ribbon of concrete still stretches between him and home, and he illuminates the journey a few feet at a time. Brief lights flashing by tell him that his fellow travelers have also acknowledged the intrusion of the night. He steadily pushes on through the dark toward the morning or home, whichever may come first.

THE ACHING had begun slowly and slightly, with spasmodic numbness in my left foot and consistent weariness which bordered on acute fatigue. The numbness I accepted as the result of long months of sitting, studying, commuting hundreds of miles every week to complete resident requirements for a Ph.D. I was certain the weariness had moved in because I had plunged without restraint into the rigorous demands of a new pastorate during the past six months.

I rationalized that strength and vitality would return if I could just get away for a small vacation, a gift of time we had not given ourselves in five years. I promised family and friends I would do just that as soon as we got some additional staff members to carry on the work.

But my body did not hear my promises, and a deteriorating system did not take my good intentions into consideration. I continued to push, to drive, to lift, to carry every burden both physical and spiritual.

Nagging, persistent, abused nerve endings kept trying to get my attention, but I kept brushing them aside as an irritated parent tries to ignore a whining child. Then, in a burst of agitation, determined that I would listen to them, the subtle symptoms recruited new forces, assembled at a central point, and struck, attempting to head me off at the pass.

It was Sunday morning, and my wife Margie and I were driving to church. The ever-present fatigue was joined by a loss of sight in my right field of vision, which blotted out the right half of billboards and signs as we drove past. Soon realizing the problem was not going away, I told Margie what was happening.

Within the ten or fifteen minutes it took to reach the church, my left arm had begun to ache deeply. Margie summoned one of our physician members to my study, and after a brief examination he assured me that it was neither my heart nor a stroke. He allowed me to preach that morning, after I made elaborate promises of restraint and brevity.

It was the first sermon I preached under extreme physical strain and anxiety, but it was not the last. For the next two years, every sermon, talk, or prayer I delivered was given either in excruciating pain, foggy weakness, or often both.

It will pass, I kept telling myself that fateful morning, and all the agonizing mornings to follow. I was particularly certain that this original visitation of deficiency was easily explained and soon to be gone.

I reminded Margie that we had just endured an exhausting weekend, physically and emotionally. We had just survived that dreaded journey that thousands of parents face each fall: we had taken our daughter Terri hundreds of miles from home to enroll in college. On the way back, we had visited our son Randy and his wife Dara for several hours, and had driven on home late Saturday night in a sweeping rainstorm.

I rationalized that any normal body would bend under such strain, and that mine would soon snap back. Always in good general health and possessing a natural resilience to pressure, I was self-confident that I could handle this thing.

But we seldom carry the keys to our own prisons, and after several days of increasing symptoms, it became obvious that I needed help beyond myself. I entered the hospital for the first of fourteen such confinements I would experience over the next two years.

Then began the long succession of tests which seemed never to end: the thumping and gouging and probing. The listening and watching and waiting. The samples and comparisons and evaluations. The X-rays and fluoroscopes and electrocardiograms and encephalograms and brain waves and brain scans and angiograms and gastroscopic probes and endless machinery. The needles and pills and foul-tasting liquids. The consultations and explanations and endless questions. The head shaking and shoulder shrugging and the starting all over again. The invasion of privacy and the worry and the expense.

I often felt I was on a nonstop treadmill and couldn't get off. Three certainties kept me going back for more. I knew I was sick. I knew I had to get well. I knew I had to trust someone.

Although the original vision impairment had subsided, a multitude of other problems had developed. I was having unbearable headaches, numbness in my face and hands, stomach cramps, sharp "electrical shock" type pain in my legs, uncontrollable muscle spasms, and deep valleys of weakness and depression.

The multiplicity of my symptoms only served to confuse the doctors more. Medical diagnoses are often similar to spiritual and social evaluations: the more definitive and localized a symptom, the more easily it is detected, identified, and treated. When the hurt is spread around, that does not make it easier to understand and get at; it only makes it more elusive and uncontrollable.

Neither does life always cooperate by simplifying itself when complications set in. In the midst of my growing physical ailments and mental anguish, my active, exciting university church was needing all the vitality and stamina a man could muster. Also, I had recently begun the writing of my doctoral dissertation, which was the first item that had to be shelved for later pursuance.

I continued, however, to function as best as possible as pastor and preacher. Months later I would develop new approaches to pastoral ministries to compensate for the restriction of conventional methods. I would also learn new ways of preaching and teaching. For the time being, though, I was more immediately concerned about being in the pulpit every Sunday to preach. Visitors were coming to hear the new pastor, new members were joining every Sunday, and I felt a deep personal responsibility to maintain the momentum.

The church had been pastorless for almost two

years, and there was an understandable need for shepherding and pastoral care. I had always been available for any call during my pastoral ministries, but in this congregation I felt the urgent need of such availability as never before.

Therefore, we kept our growing apprehensions to ourselves and shared only a minimum of facts about the physical realities. I could not bear the thought of letting this struggling, reviving church know it had a seriously ill pastor. So, during these early days of bewilderment and exploration, I stayed "on the job" except for my actual hospital confinements.

It was thus during a day of intense pain and weakness that I prepared to conduct the funeral for the beloved physician. I had told Margie several times during the morning that I did not think I could possibly do it if I didn't improve. Wanting to be with the grieving family and church at a time when they so desperately needed a pastor, I called my neurologist to help me make it.

And so I heard the dreaded diagnosis, and the night which had been creeping in with tenacious insistence would be denied no longer. My world was suddenly dark, and I did not yet have presence of mind to notice that other travelers had turned on their lights. I was too paralyzed with fear to seek my own light in the darkness.

ADJUSTING TO THE DARK

My bones are pierced in me in the night season (Job 30:17).

THE LORD JESUS said that men love darkness because their deeds are evil, indicating the protective covering of the night. But, for the same reason—the inability to see what is there—men also hate and fear the darkness.

Man thinks that if he can just see and know the size of his adversary, he will know what to do, even if he can't conquer it. "Show me my enemy's face" is the cry of warriors since antiquity. "Let me face my accuser" is the cry for justice from every indicted man.

And it is generally true that revealedness is better than hiddenness, that knowledge is preferred over ignorance, and that fact is more powerful than speculation. But it is also true that men are sometimes terrified and immobilized by what they see and hear when the veil is lifted.

"Fools rush in where angels fear to tread" may be succinctly said of those who demand answers before all the questions are in, and who attack a vast darkness with only a sliver of limited light.

I DO NOT THINK I had ever been excessively body-conscious, dwelling on the appearance, condition, and functions of my body. I was mildly grateful for health and confidently aware of normalcy, and thus able to give my attention to affairs other than my personal physique.

During the weeks of increasing symptoms, endless tests, and growing anxiety, I tried to repress thoughts about my physical problems more strongly than ever, hoping, I suppose, that they would go away if consistently ignored.

With the pronouncement of the doctor's presumptive diagnosis of multiple sclerosis, a peculiar and radical change took place immediately in my attitude toward my body. I became obsessed with observing the slightest irregularities. Common functions I had always taken for granted became the focal point of detailed inspection. I began to absorb, assimilate, and evaluate every scrap of information about multiple sclerosis, a disease I could not even correctly pronounce when I was first told I might have it.

Multiple sclerosis is a disease of the brain and spinal cord caused by an unknown agent that attacks the covering (myelin) sheath of nerve fibers, causing a temporary interruption of nerve impulses. The situation compares with stripping off the insulation around electrical wires. The protective sheath cannot be reproduced, and hard patches develop instead (sclerosis is the Latin word for scar). Multiple results occur throughout the body, depending on what part of the central nervous system has been affected. Without remission, the disease may eventually cause permanent paralysis.

It is the mystery disease of medical science. The cause is unknown and, therefore, medical treatment is indefinite and usually unsatisfactory. In the maze of uncertainties which surround the disease, perhaps the most difficult to understand and explain is the uncertainty of diagnosis. Even in the most advanced cases, we heard doctors still using the term "presumptive diagnosis."

The only absolutely certain diagnosis of MS occurs at the time of autopsy when the damage to the nerve fibers can actually be inspected. While the victim is alive, diagnosis must be made through extensive neurological testing and the patient's clinical history. Many symptoms are subjective, and the physician must depend on the patient's accuracy in describing these. Even the obvious physical symptoms which can be objectively observed can also be caused by factors other than MS. Many diseases and neurological disorders produce symptoms similar to, and sometimes identical with, those of MS.

When we learned of this vague and uncertain quality of MS, and when we heard our doctors repeatedly say they were not positive, Margie and I decided quickly to keep the diagnosis to ourselves until we were more reasonably sure that it was accurate. We did not want to alarm our family or unsettle the church unnecessarily. Neither of us had any desire for sympathy or attention over this sort of issue, and we certainly did not want to sound false alarms prematurely.

Inquiries at the local MS chapter were made in discretion and privacy. Books, magazine articles, and news items about the disease were collected secretly and read repeatedly. We began to carefully observe known victims of MS to compare their symptoms with mine. We were elated to find something strikingly different, but then depressed to read or hear again that variation itself is characteristic of the disease. We were determined to resolve the question, but, I suppose, at the same time determined to resolve it our way for a different diagnosis.

I had always been slightly critical of those who refused to accept a reputable medical opinion, and traveled near and far to hear a different diagnosis, or to discover a miracle cure. This would be one of my first preconceived notions to fall by the wayside. In months to come I would learn repeated lessons about the value of experience and the folly of judging others until you have walked where they walk.

We consulted with several other local doctors about their experience with MS patients and their reaction to the neurologist's diagnosis in my case.

They were concerned, thorough, and patient, but always evasive and unsure because of the early stage of my problem.

We heard of a popular young neurologist ninety miles away and hurriedly made an appointment to see him. After a full afternoon of examination, we were more confused than ever. He was almost positive that I did not have MS because some of my complaints were not typical of the disease, especially my excessive pain. When I spoke of this to the local neurologist, he showed me in a medical journal that sharp pain was, indeed, an occasional symptom.

After weeks of relentless pain and weakness and bewildering frustration, I consented to enter one of the nation's most renowned diagnostic clinics. Until now, I had attempted to continue my pastoral duties as effectively as possible, with a minimum of reference to my problems. Now it became necessary to explain to the church that I was going to the famous clinic to get a good thorough checkup so that I could more quickly recover my old steam.

The first visit was inconclusive and I was asked to return for a second stay. This seemed to arouse suspicion in the church that I might have a serious problem. The final report of the battery of tests was as puzzling and depressing as the previous evaluations.

I did not appear to have strong indications of some typical MS symptoms, yet there seemed to be no other explanation for the severe symptoms which I did have. In a very carefully worded summation, I was told that I might not have the disease and that eventually another cause for my trouble might be discovered, but in the meantime it looked more probable that I did have it, and should start living my life accordingly.

I do not know if it was because of such a vague and disturbing analysis, or because of the progress of my ailment, but at this time I began to exhibit extreme nervousness and irritability. I had never been very sympathetic with people whose nerves seemed on edge all the time, and I sincerely believed that anyone could control his emotions if he tried hard enough. Now my own emotions were uncontrollable and my nerves seemed about to explode. At the least provocation I found myself weeping, a reaction which was completely foreign to my formerly composed nature. For the first time, I could honestly believe people who said they "couldn't help it" when they burst into tears or screams.

There comes a time when people must trust other people, when they must share a burden which has become too heavy for one to carry alone. Out of stubbornness, or pride, or fear, or maybe all of these, I had waited too long to share the real agony that my wife and I had been bearing by ourselves. We are both private people as far as personal problems are concerned, and we do not easily go public with our hurts.

Our first responsibility, of course, was to be completely honest with our children and close members of our families. They were beautiful in their supportive warmth and encouragement. They knew practically nothing about MS, but they knew we would need all the love and understanding possible if I did have it.

Next, we invited about a dozen of our church leaders and their wives to our home, where I told them (in great nervousness and an embarrassing flow of tears) that it appeared their pastor might have a crippling, incurable disease. Without exception, they pledged their loyal support and fervent prayers in our behalf. One man expressed the gracious sentiment that just having me in the pulpit, even if I were in a wheelchair, would be sufficient. A member of the pulpit committee which had brought me to the church reminded me that they had originally told me that they did not expect the pastor to do all the work and visiting, but to specialize in studying and preaching, and that now they would fulfill their task and be my legs.

Then I told the church in a Sunday worship service. I tried to be careful and accurate in my description of my illness. When I mentioned multiple sclerosis, I tried to explain the mysterious nature of the disease and the uncertainty of the diagnosis. There were a few who were personally acquainted with MS and knew as much or more than I, but the vast majority knew practically nothing about it. As should have been expected, the news quickly spread throughout the community that I had a progressively crippling, incurable disease. Although a genuine spirit of compassion and sympathy was extended to me and my wife, a despondent aura of gloom descended on the church.

It seemed that every person I met reflected pity

for me and concern for a struggling church which needed a strong, healthy pastor. A few months before, I had felt unquestionably that I was that man they needed. Now I wasn't sure of that, or anything, anymore.

SHARING THE JOURNEY

They grope in the dark without light (Job 12:25).

HURTS COME in all sizes, and nighttime comes in various shades of darkness. Although pain is intensely personal, it is thoroughly universal. It simultaneously inflicts itself in a multitude of forms upon innumerable victims.

Because my hurt is so uniquely mine, it's really hard for me to believe that others are suffering as much as I, and yet my mind tells me it must be so.

The community of pain creates strange friendships, and those who would never be mutually attracted at other levels are drawn inexorably into a camaraderie of hurting. The bond of suffering may reflect earth's truest democracy, in which all men are equal in their pain of body and anguish of soul.

Self-pity is counterproductive in a healthy person;

but it is absolutely destructive in the physically ill. Protection against this subtle enemy comes chiefly from the simple recognition that you are not the first nor the last to pass through this valley, and that your pain, as much as you hate to admit it, is probably not the worst.

I COULD NOT REMEMBER previously knowing anyone who had multiple sclerosis. I had thought of it as a rare disease and was surprised to learn that more than 500,000 Americans are afflicted with it. I was even more surprised at the number of local people who had it, and that nearly everyone had a family member or close friend with the malady. Once the word was out that I had MS, we seemed to be deluged with telephone calls, introductions to MS patients, hundreds of case histories, well-meaning home remedies, lists of doctors and hospitals, and as always there was the constant rumor of a miracle cure.

We were advised to go to Germany, England, Russia, California, Virginia, New York. We were told to forget it, that there was no hope anywhere. We were given articles, books, recipes, health foods, and new medicines. We were discouraged and encouraged. We could not believe that so many people "knew" so much about a disease about which we were relatively ignorant.

The one redeeming trait which seemed to characterize almost every contact was sincerity. You can tolerate an awful lot of interruptions, questions, and suggestions if you feel that people really care. I do not remember being annoyed by any curiosity seekers or prying busybodies. Even advice we never intended to follow was appreciated because we knew it came from a genuine desire to help.

Long-time MS patients were the most appreciated as they opened old memory wounds I knew they would rather leave closed, as they exposed their own emotions to new hurt by telling me what lay ahead, as they bravely demonstrated their latest achievements of conquering the simplest physical obstacle, as they offered to give of themselves even though so much had been taken from them.

Identity is always a relational thing. We know who we are and what we are in relation to the significant others of our lives. It is dishonest, and sometimes cruel, to claim to identify with another unless we are openly honest about our relationship.

For years I had mumbled, "I know how you feel" in circumstances which were actually foreign to my experience. I have learned that it is more honest and even more helpful to say in such instances, "I can't imagine what you're going through, for this has never happened to me, but as your friend (pastor, teacher, etc.) I want to support you and help you through this."

But then, there are those who do know because of personal involvement, either as a patient or through a close loved one. The irony is that those who have the most to share usually say the least. They have a quiet dignity born of lonely suffering, and a compassionate look that needs no translation into words.

They may be eager to talk and willing to help, but just as often they may turn away kindly but firmly. It is too painful for them to watch a beginner take his first steps on a torturous path they have endured for years. I understood their reluctance to get involved, for I was already trying to avoid contact with them.

Well-meaning friends would try to get me together with someone who was courageously "doing so well." I knew they were wanting to show me that I could overcome if others had, but the last thing in the world I wanted was to spend an evening with a hopelessly twisted, crippled, or paralyzed MS victim who mirrored what I could expect myself to become.

The local MS chapter tried courteously and insistently to get me to attend group sessions for both physical and emotional therapy. Crusading citizens tried to enlist my "testimony" for the annual MS drive for contributions. From all of these I turned away in bitterness and sickness. My night was too fresh, my wound was too raw, and my heart was too stubborn.

I had not accepted the diagnosis. Even though I had shared it with the people of my world, I had not convinced myself that it was true. I developed a deep and permanent respect for every MS patient I met or heard about. I felt sincere gratitude for everyone who offered any kind of help. But deep inside, I kept telling myself that I was different, that I didn't really have the dread disease.

People were identifying with me with more openness than I had ever experienced. They seemed to accept me more as "one of them" because I had a serious health problem. I pondered what this might be saying about our conventional roles. Had my previous good health been a barrier between me and those who had known critical illness? Had my energetic pulpit appearance set me apart from those who had lost the zest and zeal for life?

Many questions raised in that hour have continued unanswered to this hour, but at least they have been brought into the open where they can be candidly examined. One such question concerns the relevance of physical suffering to spiritual maturity. Is it absolutely necessary for a person to be broken in body before he can be whole in spirit?

Many months later I would find myself in the depths of vocational despair and unbearable loneliness. I would catch myself asking, Where are those comforters who were concerned about the pain of my body, but offer no solace for the anguish of my soul? Then I would remind myself that this has been my failure also. Always ready to rush to the hospital or to answer a midnight distress call, I have never been too eager to get involved with those who have been misunderstood, slandered, or rejected. While giving extravagant notice to the wounds of the flesh, we conveniently ignore the deeper wounds of the spirit.

O dear God, if we could only reach across the chasms of the broken heart as quickly as we can those of the broken body! It really ought to be easier, for everyone has not been through a tragic accident or lived with an incurable disease, but everyone has known fear, failure, disappointment, rejection, confusion, and sin. Vast differences of heredity and environment will always keep us from being the ideal physical community, but we should not let anything keep us from being the spiritual community of faith, hope, and love.

And so the darkness brought new names and faces into my world. It carved out new heroes for me to admire, and it revealed a tenderness and generosity among people of all ages and all walks of life. But it also introduced new and disturbing questions, which, if ever answered, will equip us better to help those who follow in the night.

LEARNING THE ROAD

He discovereth deep things out of darkness (Job 12:22).

LIFE CAN BE LIVED either in the shallows or in the depths. Each individual decides for himself, and the criterion for that decision is mental involvement. Even the most profound situation can be lived in the shallows if one is determined not to think deeply about it, and the most common occurrence can produce a wealth of wisdom if one digs out every small nugget of meaning.

There is, however, no biased partiality in the search for deeper and greater truths. To learn more does not always mean to learn more good, for there is a depth to evil which will also be uncovered by those who sincerely seek the good. But there is a depth to good that cannot be forever strangled by superficial evil.

We human beings think that knowledge is power, that the more we know, the stronger we are. In many ways, this is so, but it is also the experience of life that "in much wisdom is much grief: and he that increaseth knowledge increaseth sorrow" (Ecclesiastes 1:18).

With a foreboding premonition of such a warning, many deliberately choose not to learn more for fear of hurting more. They honestly believe that "what they don't know won't hurt them." But others cannot tolerate ignorance and are determined to know everything, even if the knowledge itself becomes a new pain.

FROM SEVERAL DIFFERENT SOURCES we began to hear about a highly reputable medical team which was having noteworthy success in the treatment of MS patients. The team was headed by a renowned doctor and professor of neurology who wrote textbooks on the subject.

Praying for wisdom to know what to do and the means with which to do it, we accepted as divine answer the timely offer of private plane availability and the encouragement of close friends in that distant city.

I became a human guinea pig, entering into a carefully supervised experimental program for the treatment of multiple sclerosis. Of course, I was nervous, even a little frightened, but I was impelled by the recent answers to prayer in this direction, the reputation of the man in charge, the growing acceptance of the seriousness of my condition, and the sustaining faith that God was in control.

Almost immediately the internationally known physician gave a strong diagnosis of multiple sclerosis and began the series of tests and treatments which he used for dozens of MS patients in the program. Other members of the medical team, nurses, and improving patients all assured me that I was doing the right thing and was in the best hands in the business.

I made several subsequent flights back and forth for more treatments, more tests, and more instruction on how to live as an MS victim. I was repeatedly told that the sooner I completely accepted the diagnosis, the better my body would respond to treatment, but I could not make myself believe that I really had MS. For one thing, I was not responding positively to the treatments which were helping so many others. In fact, they seemed in some ways to be more damaging than helpful. Also, I continued to develop a great variety of other problems which kept me on a constant round of specialists and examination rooms.

Since I was being treated in one of the world's leading medical centers, it was convenient (and very expensive) to have all of these secondary problems and worrisome symptoms checked out. Each test revealed that I did have some problem in that area, but not severe enough to mimic the symptoms of MS. The only connection seemed to be the repeated reminder that MS affects so many areas of the body, inducing impairment of vision, speech, hearing, bladder control, equilibrium, muscle coordination, and many other functions. So I was brought back again and again to be told that I was a classic MS victim.

One hopeful, though frightening, possibility for a different diagnosis occurred when I started having unusual symptoms in the chest and severe spells of weakness. One doctor ventured to suggest that I might have a left atria mexoma, which is a small tumor on the inside of the heart. To ascertain the existence of such a tumor would mean expensive, painful, and dangerous tests including a heart catherization. If such a tumor did exist, it would mean open heart surgery, something I definitely did not anticipate with pleasure. When I was told, however, that such a tumor could cause some of the same symptoms as MS, and that there was a slight possibility that the MS diagnosis could be overruled, I agreed to the tests. Even dangerous surgery sounded more palatable than a crippling, incurable disease.

We told no one but our family and closest friends of this new possibility. The church thought I was merely returning to the center for more routine treatments. The doctors understood my obligations, and had considerately worked out a schedule so that I could always be back with the church on Sunday. This trip appeared no different, and as far as results were concerned, it wasn't.

The tests were, as we had been warned, very thorough, very painful, and very expensive. They were also very clear in determining that I had a strong, healthy heart with absolutely no left atria mexoma or other malfunction. With terribly mixed emotions, I thanked God for such an encouraging report about my heart, but went into a long spell of depression over the realization that I was back again to the diagnosis of MS.

Now I began to more actively seek out MS patients to compare their symptoms with mine, to ask endless, tedious questions about what to expect. My probing was surely uncomfortable for them and totally unprofitable for me. I learned that no two MS patients are alike, and comparing symptoms is a fruitless waste of time. I learned that what brings relief to one is ineffective for another. I became an avid reader of medical journals which dealt with the subject and snatched at every news item which hinted at a breakthrough.

I had been determined to get the best medical opinion possible. I felt I had gotten it, and all earlier diagnoses had been confirmed, but I was not satisfied. I was obsessed with learning everything I could about MS, but was always left feeling new emptiness along with new knowledge. Was the dissatisfaction and emptiness due to despair because I knew I had MS, or to frustration because I could not believe that this darkness was mine?

HEARING THE GUIDE

For God speaketh . . . in a vision of the night (Job 33:14, 15).

MAN HAS ALWAYS YEARNED to hear the voice of God, to know with certainty that an all-powerful Supreme Being is in control of the universe, and that he is disposed toward man as the Heavenly Father of love and providential care.

We listen for his whispering in the wind, his shouts in the storm, and his greetings in the morning freshness. We look for his footprints in the sands of time and his words in the book of life. We seek his reflection in the faces of those we like and search out his wisdom in truths that are pleasurable.

It is difficult for us to believe that a God of peace would use instruments of conflict as vehicles of his message. Why would the Creator of light condescend to work in the dark, and why would he choose the night in which to speak a word that men yearn to hear in the day?

We forget that darkness and light are man's limitations and boundaries, not God's. It is all the same world to him. The setting of the sun does not affect the Almighty's vision or purpose. The psalmist had discovered this truth about God, and exclaimed it in poetic prayer: "Yea, the darkness hideth not from thee; but the night shineth as the day: the darkness and the light are both alike to thee" (Psalm 139:12).

Those who cringe in fear of the dark because they cannot see are heartened to know that the Heavenly Father sees everything as clearly as though it were noonday. Those who are frightened by strange noises in the night should listen carefully lest they miss hearing the voice of God himself.

THESE DAYS OF DARKNESS were not all filled with despair. There were sharp bursts of hope that sprang up suddenly like a covey of quail fluttering in the hunter's face. There were deep rivers of faith that overran their banks and soaked every event in the vicinity. There was the warm sunlight of love that burned away the germs of bitterness and resentment. Some of these supportive virtues came surprisingly from our own reservoir of spiritual strength which turned out to be deeper than we would have thought; but most of them came from the amazing variety and number of dear people who allowed God to speak his messages through them.

He spoke to my loneliness by assuring me that literally thousands really cared. This message came week after week on the wings of news that a group here and a group there was praying, that churches of our faith and some of other faiths were having special prayer meetings for us, that individuals were offering to do anything humanly possible to help.

He spoke to me of Christian fellowship as deacons and other members bridged the gap left wide by my increasing inability to minister. Local pastors met for prayer and sent word that they would take turns in meeting pastoral obligations I could not, without expense to me or the church. Administrative and faculty personnel in our university offered to assume practical duties at the church. Community groups were ready to help supply physical aids if they became necessary.

He spoke to me of his knowledge of my mundane needs and his ability to meet those needs. In an uncanny, almost eerie timing, money was somehow available at the eleventh hour when we had to have it. Private planes were offered for our transportation, and there always seemed to be someone waiting at the end of each journey with a room, or a meal, or a prayer.

He spoke to me of the gentleness, kindness, patience, and understanding of common people. When I had to sit on a stool to preach every sermon for over a year, not a person frowned or said a critical word. When I had to be helped to walk from the funeral coach to the grave many times, the family deep in its own grief was always considerate of my inconvenience. Young couples were beautifully cooperative in rearranging wedding ceremonies so that I would not have to stand too long in one place. Some even had to be especially understanding when a severe attack would prostrate me at the last minute, causing them to have to continue with a substitute preacher.

He spoke to me of different methods of ministry that he could use through me. Always an active visitor, I now had to reserve my strength for preaching and could not make the accustomed rounds of visiting hospital patients, shut-ins, members with critical needs, and prospects for church membership. I began to rely on the telephone as a constant contact with these groups, and I was happily surprised at their acceptance of the idea and their appreciation that I had made the effort. More time at home gave me time to write daily those who needed a word from the pastor. My weekly column in our church paper became a strong and vital link between me and the people as I poured out my deepest feelings in writing. Staff members at the church were cooperative in assuming responsibilities that I had always reserved for the pastor, and were quite willing to assemble for staff meetings in my home when I could not go to the church. Laymen were entrusted with important committee work which I had been sure could not prosper without me. In dozens of ways, God was telling me that his work would go on, with or without me, and that there are many different ways to minister.

He spoke to me of the comfort and encouragement that comes from human communication. Cards and letters poured in from around the country. Frequent long-distance phone calls convinced us that former church members and old friends had not forgotten us. Such spontaneous and unexpected contacts prodded my own guilty conscience to make new resolutions. How often I had neglected to communicate my concern for someone who was ill or in sorrow, with the flimsy excuse that they knew how I felt or that they wouldn't miss my greeting with all the others flowing in. Now I knew that neither excuse was valid, that any kind of contact is better than an assumption with good intentions, and I vowed to be more responsive to the pain of others.

He spoke to me of the vitality and reality of answered prayer, but he taught me how to recognize answers I was not expecting. I learned anew to leave the method and means of the answer in God's hands. My suggestions to him for implementing a prayer request were limited by my knowledge of resources, while his vast knowledge knew every resource.

The natural inclination of prayer was to ask the Father to miraculously remove the disease from my body—to make me well again. The Spirit of God would not let me pray this prayer of the yearning flesh (read Romans 8:26). With pragmatic realism I knew that if the disease of multiple sclerosis were indeed in my body, my prayers should be petitions for coping with it, not wishes that it had never happened.

My primary prayer, underlying all secondary requests, was that God would enable me to complete the task he had put me on earth to do. I imagined that this might mean preaching from a wheelchair. I imagined that it might mean writing, and eventually dictating, from my bed. I imagined devices that could be built to assist me in carrying on a productive life as an invalid. I imagined the possibility of long remissions, which often come to MS victims, but so far had shown no signs of coming to me. I imagined new kinds of ministries and new ways of serving, but never once did I imagine the specific answer to my prayers which eventually came. My basic, primary prayer was answered in fullness beyond my imagination, reminding me that we do not have to instruct the Great Physician how to do his job once we have placed ourselves in his hands.

He spoke to me of patience for the long journey and acceptance of the present moment. "One day at a time" became a calming formula for self-preservation. Somehow the Spirit of Love protected me from agonizing speculations of "what if . . ." Somehow I instinctively knew the wisdom of the Master's words, "Take therefore no thought for the morrow: for the morrow shall take thought for the things of itself. Sufficient unto the day is the evil thereof" (Matthew 6:34).

He was speaking to me in the night, and the knowledge of his presence was my promise for tomorrow.

TWO

...running from the dawn...

Let the stars of the twilight thereof be dark;
let it look for light, but have none;
neither let it see the dawning of the day.

Job 3:9

DETOURING UNDER PROTEST

They . . . rebel against the light . . . for the morning is to them even as the shadow of death (Job 24:13, 17).

THERE ARE CREATURES of the forest which hunt, eat, and mate during the night, and are never seen after the first ray of sunrise. Tiny animals and insects emerge bravely under cover of dark to prowl through a building, and are seen scurrying frantically for a hiding place when sudden light is flashed on them.

Human beings consider themselves creatures of light, despising the darkness, and greeting the day by stretching toward the sun. But this is the spirit of man and a reflection of the Spirit of God—"in the image of God created he him."

When the body begins to overpower the spirit, man slowly, unconsciously, begins to prefer the dark over the light. The more obsessed he becomes with the needs and desires and afflictions of his physical nature, the more he acquires the habits and inclinations of the animal world.

If light comes in the form of intolerable facts, he may rebel against the light with a shield of contradictions which he desperately prays will be strong enough to ward off the coming blow. Or, if his rational self overrules his emotional self, convincing him of the reality of unwanted things revealed by the advancing light, he may instinctively run from the dawn.

IT WAS A VERY SIMPLE, little moment that lasted no more than ten seconds, but it was the emotional trigger that released the flow of rational truth into my stubborn heart. The best professional authorities in three outstanding medical centers had not been able to convince my nervous system and emotional reflexes that I really had multiple sclerosis. The renowned specialist who had me in his experimental treatment program seemed so thorough and so positive about the diagnosis that I felt rather ridiculous for even questioning him. Yet there was an inner core of hope that would not submit.

Then, one day back home, Margie suggested that we go for a drive in the beautiful late afternoon. The fresh spring air and the sparkling green of nature everywhere seemed to be just the tonic my depressed spirit needed. Then I saw them: a grandfather playing ball with his grandson on the front lawn of their home. It was an everyday, common neighborhood tableau, but it flared into a drama of tragic portent in my mind.

Before I could stop the words, they exploded from my mouth: "I'll never be able to do that!" Thinking it meant I had recognized the remote possibility, but saying it seemed to crystallize it into a reality. I immediately started trembling and crying, and asked Margie to take me home. I was frightened by the inability to control my emotions almost as much as I had been by the realization of being an invalid. Together, both phenomena sent me into a deep period of despondency, and I found myself believing the doctors for the first time.

Little things are of greater importance in our lives than we can possibly imagine. Little decisions take up much more time and deliberation than the big issues of life. Little criticisms take a much heavier toll on our health and happiness than long hours of hard labor. Little remembrances speak more eloquently of true love than expensive gifts. The loss of little privileges may tear our world apart more viciously than the loss of great prestige and power.

I had already begun to accept the fact that my days as a public leader were probably limited, if not over. I had been trying to adjust to a change in our style of ministering and living that seemed inevitable. I was resigned to taking a lesser role in world affairs, regardless of the nature of the ailment that was causing me to be sidelined. But I evidently had not steeled myself for the shock that even small pleasures would be taken away.

Our children are our most valuable possessions, and God's most beautiful gift to our lives. We have loved and cherished every day of every stage of their growth. We have shared their laughter and their tears, their victories and their failures. We have worked with them, worshiped with them, studied with them, played with them, and grown with them. I always placed one of their school events, or piano recitals, or birthday parties on the same level of importance for scheduling as church or civic functions. We belonged to them without reservation or qualification, and thanked God daily for whatever part of their lives we were privileged to share.

How deeply this common bond of family sharing had penetrated was revealed in striking clarity that afternoon. I literally went to pieces when I thought I would never be able to romp and play with my grandchildren as I had with my children. I felt a sense of being deprived, even robbed, that I had not known before. I felt that some basic inalienable right had been violated. A man may acquire money, position, and power, but not consider them fundamental rights and can, therefore, survive their loss. But he can barely live without those cherished treasures he has subconsciously held as being fundamental—such as playful frolic with a laughing child.

For several months I had been walking with the aid of a cane, a distasteful necessity. I had never given much thought to the mental anguish or social embarrassment that people experience when forced to use a cane or wheelchair. Now I would always be sensitive to the feelings of others in this predicament. Still, I had not realized the seriousness of such impairment until the days of despondency following the episode with the grandfather and the child.

Whereas I had previously avoided such thoughts, I now began enumerating the various things I already could not do and worrying about how many other disabilities I would incur. Simple activities once taken for granted were now on the scale of major athletic events. Margie and I had always enjoyed walking together in late evening, and now circling the block was a herculean feat which often ended in pain and frustration.

As a young man I had participated in a few athletic pursuits such as track, basketball, and boxing, and had remained an avid fan of spectator sports such as football and baseball. Watching these events now, either in person or on television, I caught myself bitterly asking why some were blessed with abundant health and strength, only to be squandered in pleasure, while some just wanted ordinary health to serve God and humanity, and were handicapped.

Knowing there was no answer to such futile questions, I tried to turn away from seeing the big difference between me and the vigorously active. The sports page did not interest me as before, and the presence of healthy young people was more of an irritation than I ever revealed to anyone. I felt uncomfortable with either the vitality of youth which I had so recently possessed, or the deterioration of the sick and elderly which I was so rapidly approaching. I belonged to neither world and yet I had visited both.

I saw what I was becoming and wanted no part of it. I never contemplated ending my life, and yet I developed an understanding sympathy for those who did harbor such dark impulses. I had always boasted that I could handle any problem as long as I knew its name and nature. Now that knowledge was the very thing that was debilitating me.

I quit reading the books and articles about MS. I don't know if I was trying to say that these didn't involve me, or assuming that I was beyond help. I only know that I felt I knew too much already, that additional information would just add more bars to my prison.

I learned a deep and penetrating lesson about human nature, which, of course, I could recognize and evaluate only months later in retrospect. One must emerge from a tunnel before he can look back and survey the meanings of the engulfing darkness of that journey.

The lesson concerned the indispensable element of hope for any human situation. Knowledge is not only useless, it is bitterly resented if it cannot be applied with overtures of hope. What did I care about becoming an expert on multiple sclerosis if I could see no hope for anything but a worsening condition? I was given several new books on prayer, but why should I want to read new devotional thoughts about prayer if God was not going to answer my prayers?

Later I would remember these hopeless feelings

and remind myself that preaching and teaching are worthless exercises if they do not have the underlying theme of hope. But in that valley, I found I could do nothing more than the very thing I resented in others—I kept preaching facts and doctrines I sincerely believed, but without the music of hope ringing in them.

I was running from the very dawn which I tried to get others to accept. I was imploring sinners to admit the lostness of their souls, but I could not admit the lostness of my life's purpose. I sought to comfort those in sorrow by reminding them of God's real presence in a real world, but I could not face the reality of my own future.

The grace of God used my fumbling, half-hearted ministrations, and many said my pastoral care seemed more compassionate than before. Compassionate, yes, for I really did hurt for the hurting as never before, but I camouflaged a hopeless heart of despair with an unprecedented outpouring of biblical instruction. The wisdom of the Spirit of God mercifully reserved the knowledge of the hopeless heart to himself, and uniquely blessed the Scripture lessons to individual needs.

I never doubted the existence of God, nor his goodness and wisdom. My negative attitude had to do solely with my own limited strength to face the dawning of a new kind of world I had to somehow learn to live in. I tried to appear brave for my family and friends, but in the middle of the night God and I knew how scared I was.

CROSSING THE DESERT

Why is light given to a man whose way is hid, and whom God hath hedged in? (Job 3:23).

NATURE ABHORS a vacuum, and sets about at once to fill it with the materials at hand. Life demands and will have something at its center. Anything that diminishes the center and creates the vacuum is considered waste.

Lack of purpose is the waste of the human vacuum. Man was not made simply to exist, but to exist *for* something: to "have dominion over . . . all the earth" (Genesis 1:26). In decreeing this preeminence of man, his Creator ordained that he should "be fruitful, and multiply, and replenish the earth, and subdue it" (Genesis 1:28).

This divine call to creativity, productivity, industry, and conquest burns in the soul of every normal human being. Take away the ability or opportunity to fulfill this call, and life loses its center and a terrible vacuum settles in.

Despair comes not so much from being deprived of more, but from not being able to use what we already have. Why has the light of dawn come to a man "whom God hath hedged in"?

SINCE CHILDHOOD I have been consciously aware of my humble, though godly, heritage. Our family was a church family, and remains so to this day. Three of the four boys are ordained ministers, the fourth a deacon, and our sister a church musician. Our father was a deacon, and our mother was always active in Sunday school and mission work.

Growing a Christian family is not easy or accidental, and going to church is not the end of it. Our parents had to somehow feed and clothe the five small children during the Depression, often on $1.00 a day laborer's wages. The emotional effects of those penny-pinching years are still with us all. My two older brothers served in the military during World War Two, and our family endured wartime conditions and aftereffects, as did nearly every family in America.

In all these exposures to the realities of life, my young mind was expanding along with my growing body. I began at an early age to dream of a better world and my part in making it possible. At the age of nine I had a deeply impressive conversion experience as I committed not just my "soul" but my whole life to Christ for both salvation and service.

It seems that I always instinctively knew that I

would be a preacher. When I was twelve years old, I publicly "surrendered" to the ministry. In later years, when close friends would ask me when I was "called" to preach, I would answer, half-jokingly, that I wasn't called to preach, I was born to preach. I suppose I was trying to express how very deeply I felt that the whole reason for my existence was to proclaim the Word of God.

I did actually start preaching rather regularly in my early teens, had my first church job as a youth director at seventeen, and was ordained and pastoring my first church at eighteen.

Naturally, I continued to pursue the normal educational processes during this time, graduating from high school and entering college in my hometown. By the time I had received my college degree (in six years rather than four) I was married, had one child, and was pastoring a relatively large church full time. Because of these responsibilities I did not go on immediately to graduate school or seminary as did most of my classmates. Instead, I continued to pastor and was privileged to serve some of the finest churches one could hope for.

Fifteen years after graduating from college, I decided to extend my formal education into Master's and doctoral programs. I had attended several summer institutes in recent years, but had not had the time or conviction to pursue a degree program. However, in addition to pastoring, I had become quite involved in writing and had already published seven or eight books. I was beginning to feel a real need to go deeper into theological studies, and was acutely aware of my limited training.

I had no particular vocational goals in mind, other than pastoring, but I had a strong compulsion to equip myself better in order to be ready for any eventual calling of God. When I began the Ph.D. program I was pastoring a church of 3,400 members, located 250 miles from the school which I had to attend two days a week. The church was generously cooperative, and my family was encouraging and supportive.

Over the next several years, a change in pastorates was made, and our children were becoming very active teenagers. At a time when they needed more money, more understanding, and more time with father than ever, I was sandwiching in a difficult and expensive program of doctoral studies. But they were absolutely great, never complaining and always supportive of my goals, cheering me on with every decent grade.

Church leaders, school officials and professors, family and friends all performed one enabling act after another to make my academic dream a reality. Every problem, whether monetary, personal, or vocational, was saturated with prayer and appropriately answered. Completing this degree program seemed to be the clearest leading of God's will and purpose for my life that I had known in a long time. When I would periodically try to drop out, events would irresistibly turn me back again to this task.

After I had completed all my resident studies, passed the qualifying exams, and started on the writing of my dissertation, I was extended a call to pastor the university church in my hometown, across the street from my alma mater, and only a few blocks from where I had grown up as a boy. I was impressed by the possibilities of the campus ministry, challenged by the larger community potential, and stirred by the struggling church's need for a rebuilding program. They had been without a pastor for two years, and reached out eagerly for our leadership.

The first six months of our new pastorate in the old hometown were successful almost to the point of being sensational. Attendance and offerings increased dramatically, and new members were joining every Sunday. The excited church insisted that I seek out whatever new staff members I needed to help us. The city and surrounding area had been so cordial in welcoming me back that I often said that I had refuted Thomas Wolfe, that there are places where you can go home again.

Additional preaching invitations, denominational responsibilities, and writing assignments increased beyond my ability to accept. In every way it appeared that our happiest and most productive days were about to begin. We saw no end to the possibilities of our church, and the reception on our college campus had already exceeded my dreams. We bought a beautiful "permanent" home on a lovely lake at the edge of town, and felt that we had finally come to the place for which God had been preparing us.

Then, suddenly and irrevocably, I was stricken with the illness which gradually took me further and further away from realizing the potential of our ministry. In fact, whereas I had been striving for maximum possibilities, now I was desperately trying to hold on to perform the barest minimum service. Not only had a dream ended, it had been replaced by a nightmare.

When it began to dawn on me that I was critically, perhaps incurably ill, I reacted as naturally as many others have by turning away rebelliously from this glaring, unsparing, bright light of truth. My running from the dawn was punctuated and characterized by the repeated question, Why this waste?

I saw a church confused, unsettled, and for most practical purposes, leaderless. I had felt the strong hand of God moving me to become their leader, and now I was physically unable to maintain the pace they needed. Why this waste?

I saw young people everywhere, with energy waiting to be challenged and channeled, with young minds eager to learn and follow. One of my principal reasons for coming to this place was to work with college students as well as local youth, and now I couldn't even attend their events, let alone participate. Why this waste?

My degree program was almost complete, lacking only the dissertation and final orals. I had grown immeasurably in academic and theological knowledge, and felt that I was just beginning to get real substance in my preaching and writing. Now I was so weak and despondent I had neither the physical strength nor emotional will to continue my dissertation or to write anything. Why this waste?

I had felt since I was a child that I was "born to preach." I had come back to a place where preaching was both needed and responded to. I felt better satisfied with my ability and philosophy of preaching than ever before. But I experienced inundating weak spells and distracting pain every time I tried to preach, making every sermon a heartbreaking agony. Why this waste?

I knew at the time that I was not the first, nor the last to feel wasted. I had counseled hundreds with this very problem. I knew that every man feels that he is being unfairly wasted when his life's work is cut short by disease, or death, or failure. What I did not know until I experienced it was the intensely personal feeling of waste.

I tried to remind myself of all the courageous young men who had been tragically killed in wars, many of whom were already preparing for splendid careers of service to mankind. I tried to think about the beautiful young girls who had been robbed by untimely tragedy of ever being wives or mothers. I honestly tried to be sensible and logical, and tried to accept myself as another member of the vulnerable human race.

I learned, however, in an indelible lesson, that no one ever feels the waste of another life like that of his own. You can tell a man all day long that he is no different, that others are as bad off or worse than he, but that will never rebuild the shattered dreams that have been uniquely his. He knows that he has but one life to live, and if he is cut short of realizing that which makes life meaningful for him, then it is all loss, vacuum, and waste.

Perhaps, then, the better solace is not to compare

such a man's lot with another, but to help him develop a new meaning and purpose which may be even brighter than this hated dawn from which he runs.

ASKING FOR DIRECTIONS

If I be wicked, why then labour I in vain? (Job 9:29).

GOD AND SATAN fought for Job's soul, and Job suffered horribly as they fought. Thieves ravaged him and lightning killed his flocks. A hurricane blew down his house and killed his seven sons. He was smitten with boils from head to foot. His wife mocked his faith, telling him to curse God and die. His friends wounded his heart, accusing him of gross sin, the only reasonable explanation for such unprecedented suffering.

Job would not accept their indictment. He admitted that he was a sinner as other men (Job 7:20), but refused to believe that he was evil enough to have brought all this on. He took his case to God: "Thou knowest that I am not wicked" (10:7). God did, indeed, know the quality of Job's character. At the beginning, he had said to Satan, "Hast thou considered my servant Job, that there is none like him in the earth, a perfect and an upright man, one that feareth God, and escheweth evil?" (1:8).

But being and doing good was not enough to protect Job from devastating tragedy. As he reminisced about his troubles, he recalled that he was in the very acts of consolation and benevolence when his world caved in: "Did not I weep for him that was in trouble? Was not my soul grieved for the poor? When I looked for good, then evil came unto me" (30:25, 26).

Job was not the first, nor the last of earth's pilgrims to learn that neither religion nor goodness makes a person immune from trouble and trial. Faith does not keep bad things from happening to us; but it does create a new dimension of strength and purpose. Job's faith did not protect him physically, and neither did it give intellectually satisfying answers to his critics; but it did enable him to exclaim triumphantly, "Though he slay me, yet will I trust in him" (13:15).

WITH THE DAWNING consciousness that my illness was real and possibly permanent, there came also the awareness that the question of sin and suffering was also real, not just theoretical. Academic questions for intellectual exercise become vital, relevant issues when baptized in the fire of personal experience.

Even if I personally had no problem with God's

justice and goodness, I had the problem of other people bringing the issue to me. Many asked why I thought a righteous God would cause, or allow, one of his servants working for the Kingdom to be sidelined this way.

The question "Why me?" asked in the midst of trial, usually means, "What have I done so bad as to deserve this treatment?" If there are those who see themselves as truly pure enough to ask such a question, I must leave that between them and God, but I cannot honestly ask it of myself.

If physical suffering is, indeed, providentially inflicted because of specific sins, I should have been asking "Why *not* me?" years ago. I know for a fact that I have been spared greater pain and anguish endured by much purer and more innocent people than I.

If physical suffering is, instead, a natural process of what it means to be human, I should also have been asking "Why *not* me?" I am a human being, living in a physical world of cause and effect. In spite of my religious commitment or my moral status, my body does not wear an invisible shield or possess an unnatural immunity. A part of the price I pay for living is the universal susceptibility to the "thousand natural shocks that flesh is heir to."

Why, then, are we human beings so preoccupied with the ancient question of whether human suffering is divine punishment for personal sin?

Perhaps we instinctively link suffering and sin because they are the two most "real" experiences of our human pilgrimage, causing the most intense emotional responses.

Perhaps we see them as partners of destiny because they are both negative aspects of life, both pulling us down into depression, guilt, and fatalism.

Perhaps we think that physical punishment must accompany our sins, because we remember so clearly the sequence in the pattern of our childhood discipline.

Perhaps we strangely desire a tangible, even if painful, means to purge our conscience and absolve our guilt.

Perhaps we have misunderstood the biblical terms of chastisement and retribution as applying only to the physical self.

Whatever our reasons for asking it, the question is there, and the painful light of dawn only makes it more pronounced and more demanding of attention. A study of the Scriptures reveals that the question is as old as the ancients. The Bible does not evade the burning issue of unexplained suffering.

Habakkuk saw the oppression of God's people and cried, "O Lord, how long shall I cry, and thou wilt not hear! even cry out unto thee of violence, and thou wilt not save!" (Habakkuk 1:2). Though he waited in his tower for the desired response, Habakkuk had to be satisfied with the simple answer, "the just shall live by his faith" (2:4). Simple, and yet it became the hallmark of Paul's theology (see Romans 4:3) and the watchword of Luther during the Reformation.

The psalmist dealt with the same problem as he complained, "I was envious at the foolish, when I saw the prosperity of the wicked" (Psalm 73:3). He received no concrete explanation, but found peace in trusting worship: "I went into the sanctuary of God; then understood I their end" (v. 17). His ultimate response was one of faith, not knowledge: "I have put my trust in the Lord God" (v. 28).

The writer of Ecclesiastes wrestled with the apparent injustices of life. He was indignant that "there is a just man that perisheth in his righteousness, and there is a wicked man that prolongeth his life in his wickedness" (Ecclesiastes 7:15). He thought it was grossly unfair that "all things come alike to all: there is one event to the righteous, and to the wicked; to the good and to the clean, and to the unclean" (9:2). Yet, without ever discovering the key to the puzzle, he came to believe that "though a sinner do evil an hundred times, and his days be prolonged, yet surely I know that it shall be well with them that fear God" (8:12).

The prophet Jeremiah prayed, I know you are righteous, Lord, but I must ask you: "Wherefore doth the way of the wicked prosper? Wherefore are all they happy that deal very treacherously?" (Jeremiah 12:1). After a lifetime of personal persecution and national desolation, Jeremiah wrote to the captives in Babylon, assuring them that God had not forgotten them: "For I know the thoughts that I think toward you, saith the Lord, thoughts of peace, and not of evil, to give you an expected end" (29:11).

Jesus encountered the same philosophy of suffering being the result of sin. As he and his disciples saw a blind man, they turned and asked him, "Master, who did sin, this man, or his parents, that he was born blind?" (John 9:2). Jesus replied, "Neither hath this man sinned, nor his parents: but that the works of God should be made manifest in him" (v. 3). Whatever else he might have been saying, it is clear that Jesus did not accept the theory that all suffering is punishment for specific sins.

Earlier he had spoken of God's impartiality in the physical world: "He maketh his sun to rise on the evil and on the good, and sendeth rain on the just and on the unjust" (Matthew 5:45). The testimony of Christ himself confirms that goodness in itself can keep neither the sun nor the rain from the human experience.

He elaborated on this theme when he asked, "Or those eighteen, upon whom the tower in Siloam fell, and slew them, think ye that they were sinners above all men that dwelt in Jerusalem? I tell you, Nay: but, except ye repent, ye shall all likewise perish" (Luke 13:4, 5).

If goodness alone provided an invisible armor, the stones of the falling tower would have bounced off righteous men. In such a world, germs would die when they came in contact with good people, and the law of gravitation would be revoked to keep Christians from falling off cliffs.

Obviously, such an unstable, unpredictable world would lead to chaos, rampant confusion, and false professions of religion. In fact, there may be countless instances of such false professions in every generation because of the human compulsion to escape pain.

Does this mean there is no relationship between

suffering and sin? Not at all, for there is indissoluble connection between body, mind, and soul. It is just that we often misinterpret the connection. For example, there is undisputed relationship between the abuse or neglect of our body and resulting illness or infirmity. The effect can be traced from a definite cause, and if such cause is our own fault, we are childish and unfair to blame God. A friend complained bitterly because God had "given" his father lung cancer, but his father was a chain-smoker for years, ignoring his doctor's warnings.

Perhaps the most meaningful relationship between suffering and sin is one hardly ever considered, and that is the reverse of the cause and effect process. In other words, rather than sin causing suffering, many times suffering causes sin. The vital aspect of our relation with God is not so much what happens to us, but how we react to what happens.

Does our pain cause us to lose faith? Paul said that "whatsoever is not of faith is sin" (Romans 14:23). Does our life of misery cause us to resent and despise those who are better off? We are cautioned that "he that despiseth his neighbour sinneth" (Proverbs 14:21). Do we react to our bad situation with childish petulance and immature judgment? Scripture says that even "the thought of foolishness is sin" (Proverbs 24:9). Does our obsession with our own needs keep us from reaching out to help others? "Therefore to him that knoweth to do good, and doeth it not, to him it is sin" (James 4:17).

There are innumerable ways in which we can sin by our response to misfortunes. Perhaps none is so blatant, and yet so tempting, as to assume a self-righteous attitude. A suffering person sometimes feels that he is not subject to the same rules as healthy people. He may become cruel or insolent or outright immoral, and feel perfectly justified because he has already "paid his dues" in pain. This is a treacherous trap for "if we say that we have no sin, we deceive ourselves, and the truth is not in us" (1 John 1:8). One of the clearest messages in the Bible is the universality of sin, that no person, regardless of position, age, or even health, is guiltless before God (Psalm 53:3; Proverbs 20:9; Isaiah 53:6; Romans 3:23).

There are, of course, many Scripture verses which speak of chastisement by God, and these should not be ignored. On the other hand, they should be examined carefully. The Heavenly Father knows how to discipline each of his children with the various needed tools of punishment, trial, instruction, or experience. It is dangerous for the children to assume they know as much or more than the Father. They must not jump to conclusions as to the "why" of difficult happenings. It is much more constructive to be concerned with "what" God wants us to do next.

My own crucible of pain has reaffirmed for me the folly of expecting insulation from danger just because I am involved in religious work. Night comes to me, not necessarily because I am bad or good, but because I am human; and the price I must pay for my human existence is the vulnerability of the flesh.

I do not hesitate to ask my questions about good

and evil and the meaning of suffering. I am in good company when I do, for these are among the major themes of the Bible. Yet I find better use of time in asking what I am to do since it has happened, rather than demanding to know why it happened.

Although a Christian, I must not ask for personal favoritism or special treatment. I must serve my Lord out of love and gratitude, but never for divine protection from harm. How could I possibly expect such preferential treatment above him who was tried in all points as we are, and who "humbled himself, and became obedient unto death, even the death of the cross"! (Philippians 2:8).

WATCHING FOR HAZARDS

The stones of darkness, and the shadow of death (Job 28:3).

STONES IN THE PATH may be minor inconveniences in the daytime, but they become dangerous stumbling blocks in the night.

The wise traveler removes as many of the stones as he can while he can see them. If he must come this way again at night, he has protected himself by prudent preparation. If he never returns himself, he has been considerate in clearing the way for those who follow, knowing full well that previous travelers have made his journey easier.

Some stones are small, almost unnoticeable, and can be easily kicked aside. Because of their smallness, however, they are often ignored and become irritating gravel in the shoe of the weary traveler. In the dark they can be as perilous as marbles to walk upon, creating instability and uncertainty.

Some large stones are too heavy to move alone. They require assistance, perhaps teamwork, and sometimes huge machinery to be removed. But they are liabilities and impediments, and if they can be removed, even though at great expense and tedious effort, all available energy must be expended to do so.

Some stones are huge, immovable boulders. They are there to stay. The traveler can curse them, beat upon them, and waste all his days in this one spot trying to move the immovable. Or he can recognize the size and permanence of the rock, salute it as a sentinel of the night, rest in its shade in the daytime heat, use it as a landmark by which to chart his course, and go around it to discover other open paths ahead.

I DO NOT ENJOY conflict. I respond best to challenges by analysis, arbitration, and planning. Confronting an adversary head-on is against my nature and better judgment. Such confrontations invigorate some people; they depress and disorganize me. Yet I realize that some confrontations are inevitable in this life.

As I attempted to run from the dawning reality of my illness, I constantly confronted stones in the darkness with which I had to deal. My inclination to think, reason, and discuss was often overruled by demands for immediate action.

The healing process itself became a stone between me and a few zealous proponents of faith healing. I have always believed implicitly in the omnipotence of God, and that his complete, total power includes sovereignty over the human body. I know that God has healed and can again heal the sick, and I am well aware of Scripture verses which promise this. My faith, however, is in the nature and acts of God, not in some human personality, formula, or ritual.

My family and I were having some very precious and memorable experiences in prayer. We were also aware that hundreds of consecrated Christians were praying for me. Even in my most depressed hours, I never questioned the power of God and his righteousness, and after many years of personal and pastoral prayer experiences I had the peaceful conviction that I was communicating properly with the Father.

I could not believe that it was necessary for me to submit to the methods of groups and individuals who seemed determined to get me healed. I received telephone instructions at home, telling me what I should be doing to release God's power in my behalf. I had visitors to my office who wanted to lay hands on me and claim the victory of instant healing. I even had some come to the front of the church during the invitation and insist that I kneel there and let them heal me.

The congregation never knew of any of this, for I had no desire to expose, embarrass, or debate these who wanted to help, though in ways unacceptable to my theology and personality. I think I tried to be open, but none of them presented anything different than I had always heard. I told God repeatedly that I was willing to listen to any instruction he had for me, but I never had one second of feeling that he wanted me to try the route of human faith healers. It seemed rather ironical that those who talked the loudest about allowing the Holy Spirit to do his work would not listen when I said the Holy Spirit was leading me. These days taught me anew that we should be very careful about declaring authoritatively what the will of God is, when, in fact, it may be our own will that we are determined to accomplish.

Besides those insistent upon divine healing, there were those who felt compelled to suggest I try another doctor, another hospital, another medication, even another climate. They loved me and sincerely wanted to help, but sometimes we forget that causing doubts and undermining security can be more harmful than helpful. If we have specific recommendations involving definite evidence of better resources, we are obligated to share the good news. But if our advice is of a generally negative nature, born out of frustration and disappointment, it is probably better to keep it to ourselves than to share it with a patient who already has enough of a negative outlook to handle.

Because I did, indeed, have a bundle of negative things to bear, depression was a constant companion. Ordinarily an optimistic, gregarious person, I became almost a recluse and invariably pessimistic. The change was so pronounced as to almost be a reversal of personality. My wife and others close to me had to exercise high levels of tolerance and patience. They saw me at my worst, while the public saw the cheerful mask and forced optimism.

When I did let down around some outside the close family circle, I was often chided for my "lack of faith" and reminded that as a Christian minister I should set a better example. I was really preached to on several occasions, and no doubt I deserved it. But I learned that people who live in the valley do not profit by those who keep trying to get them to talk and dress and dance like mountain folk. Sometimes a man needs to weep, and our best ministry may be to let him cry his heart out, rather than giving him a "chin up" pep talk.

Depression is not always due to a mental outlook or spiritual condition. Sometimes it is the result of severe illness throwing the body, including the nervous system, off balance. Sometimes it is the result of strong medication. I think my depression was due to all of these: mental outlook, spiritual condition, physical illness, and strong medication.

The experimental treatment for MS included a chemotherapy for cancer and very strong doses of cortisone. The chemotherapy weakened my blood cells and caused my hair to come out more than it already had. The cortisone caused me to gain excessive weight, have residual skin problems, and experience long spells of intense weakness. Two years later I am still having occasional weak spells because of the cortisone and must carry a medic alert card to receive large doses of cortisone in case of severe accident or illness.

The physical disabilities had continued to increase

at an alarming rate. The pain was sometimes almost unbearable, and I do not remember sleeping a night through in two years without pain and medication. My personal and professional future became more bleak every day, and consequently my "spirits" sank. Depression had to be a natural result of all this, and yet people were constantly trying to get me to cheer up. Today I am not so quick to judge the faith or spiritual maturity of one in depression; for he may have some very real contributing causes that I know nothing about.

Some of the stones which loom in the night are the unscrupulous self-seekers who take advantage of the disadvantaged. Fortunately, these are very few, for the overwhelming majority of people sincerely want to help, or at least have no desire to add to your burden. Unfortunately, though, it is not always easy to identify those who are out to capitalize on your vulnerable position.

Recognizing that there are those who are insincere or selfish does not minimize or devalue the great host of beautiful people who are loyal, unselfish, unassuming, and instantly available. On the contrary, it makes them all the more valuable and appreciated.

The pebbles that one should be able to brush aside can be blown out of proportion by the tired and sensitive pilgrim. Morbid curiosity which asks members of the family about details of the latest disability should be laughed at, but sometimes it hurts too much to laugh.

The presumed freedom to pry into private lives

seems to come with the territory of serious illness. Suddenly your body becomes public property, and everybody feels entitled to see or at least hear the latest development. Even personal questions about your financial condition seem to be perfectly in order for some. These are ordinary human weaknesses, not intentionally harmful, and should be considered as such and shrugged off. The problem is, one of *my* human weaknesses is not being able to dismiss rudeness lightly.

Another of my weaknesses is an ambivalence toward the involvement of others. One day I think that no one cares, that people have gotten tired or bored with this old drag, and have deserted me. The next day I may think that they care too much and are trying to run my business for me, making decisions that rightfully belong to me. In my rational moments I know that it all just about equals out and balances itself, but in my emotional moments I feel either too much forsaken or too much possessed.

And so, the stones are always there, some small and some large. Some have been mercifully removed by kind hands that knew I could not do it alone. Some seem to have been purposefully placed there by greedy and devious hands. Some are of my own making, for which I can blame no one else.

There are many lights to help us get around the stones which will not move, but perhaps the human one which sustains the most is a ready sense of humor. This does not mean to laugh and joke at everything, but to learn to take nothing and no one (not even self) too seriously, to be able to recognize whimsical paradox and unavoidable irony, to know that in a better day this would be a thing to laugh at.

Incredibly, a person can maintain a sense of humor even in extreme pain and deep depression. His humor may sound brittle and sarcastic, but the hope of it is that somewhere deep inside he recognizes the incongruity of it all.

One must learn to laugh with the innocent child who giggles upon seeing him stumble and fall. After all, it probably is a funny sight. He must be big enough to see the humor in a grown man being waited on and sometimes talked to like a child. He must be patient and appreciative of others who practice an unpolished brand of humor in trying to help him forget. He must remember his own laughter as he watched the comic stub his toe in the dark, howling and jumping like a monkey. Then he can smile at himself when he lies flat after a losing encounter with a night stone, pick himself up, and move ahead one more step.

LOSING THE WAY

He hath broken me asunder . . . and shaken me to pieces (Job 16:12).

THE TABLE is shaken, and the vessel crashes to the floor, breaking into hundreds of pieces. Lying shattered and scattered, it is still the same substance, but it has lost its design and usefulness.

It was not a brand new vessel and had already performed many functions, but compared to many older vessels still in service, it had untold years of usefulness ahead. It belonged to that category of things not judged by age, but by service.

Other vessels nearby shudder as they realize how close they were to being in the unlucky spot. They know that they are made of the same brittle stuff and will also be shattered if they are ever jostled, or dropped, or thrown down.

Yet the broken vessel does not have to be swept up and thrown in the garbage. For those who see the value in it and have the skill to do it, reconstruction may be possible.

Fragments can be recovered, and patient hands can fasten them together again. It is a long and delicate process, and the scars and seams will always be there, and a new purpose or a new place may have to be found, but at least the vessel is back in service again.

If the fragments are too many and too small, they may have to be melted down and slung on the potter's wheel to start all over again. A similar form may emerge or a totally new design may be created, but there will be continued life and purpose.

SOME DECISIONS cannot be made until there is a reason which can no longer be ignored. Whether it is a decision regarding health, or money, or family, or job, or religion, one must feel that the move is necessary for it to be done with a sense of rightness.

Friends and family may correctly see the need long before you do, but they need to be patient until the need has become an unavoidable reality and a settled conviction in your own mental and emotional structure.

I had accepted the necessity of medication to relieve some of the symptoms, and to be a vital part of the experimental program. I had accepted the need for a cane to give me stability in walking. I had tried to accept and be grateful for thoughtful hands and strong arms that often had to steady, sometimes lift me.

But I had resisted every discussion and thought of a wheelchair, which somehow represented a permanence and finality I was not ready to accept. Of course, I wanted to be mobile, but on my own, not as an extension of some machinery. Besides, I still expected to get up and walk normally again someday.

My obstinance began to wither when I started conceding that it would be better to do my work with mechanical assistance than not at all. I had not been able to make hospital rounds in several months. I learned that there was a local doctor who not only made hospital rounds, but performed all his duties, even surgery, from a wheelchair. Perhaps I needed to rethink my stubborn position.

We started asking and reading about various kinds of wheelchairs. I received some interesting brochures about a new self-propelled cart, a sort of motor scooter, especially designed for MS patients. We compared functions and costs, and began a process to select the best we could afford. My mind had finally accepted the fact that if I continued at my present rate of deterioration I would definitely need some kind of wheelchair or cart within three months.

This led to a consideration of transportation. I had not been able to drive for over a year, and I think I had fairly well adjusted to being chauffeured, although I regretted the inconvenience it caused so many nice people. With a wheelchair or cart, I knew we would do better with a van instead of a car. I remembered vans that had been especially redesigned for such purposes, and began to look into this possibility.

I had already adjusted to being driven, so I had no serious problem with this minor limitation. I had been preaching sitting on a stool for over a year, and I knew that if I went to the wheelchair, I was already prepared to work from a sitting position. The church had been so gracious and understanding about these physical necessities that I knew they would support me in any other changes.

What I did keep worrying about was the weakness and dizziness that would not go away if I were in a wheelchair position. I might be able to physically go and do more, but I knew that I could not think clearly nor function properly as a full-time pastor. I wanted to believe that motorized machinery would really help, and I was ready to try it, but deep inside I knew that it would only be postponing the inevitable resignation from the pastorate.

What could I do vocationally and productively? All my life—education, experience, and planning—had been spent in the ministry. Even if I were to consider another kind of job, how could I perform it if I could not stay in the pastorate with all the help and consideration I was getting?

Writing had been an avocation for years, and I had already begun to think about writing full time after retirement. Was it possible that providential events were forcing me into that plan twenty years early? I knew I could not write as I should unless I could overcome the constant depression, pain, and weakness. Yet it still seemed the most likely means of financial support.

Painting had been an enjoyable hobby since childhood, and I had been fortunate enough to sell a number of paintings through the years. I naturally thought of this as a supplement to the writing, but I was afraid that people would just buy my paintings out of sympathy for me. How would I know if it were charity or popularity honestly earned? These may seem to be unimportant questions, but they become big-as-life issues when a man is trying to survive, provide for his family, and preserve his dignity.

I gratefully realized that I did have the writing and painting to fall back on, and that many thousands in my position had no such secondary resources. At the same time, I knew several MS patients who had declined to the point that they could not hold a pencil to write, or a brush to paint, and were not even capable of dictating. Would this be my eventual fate?

Regardless of what I might be able to do as an alternate vocation, there would always be the trauma of having to relinquish the pulpit. The most certain conviction of my life was that I was called (or born) to preach. I had found it difficult to understand and relate to those who, sincerely wanting to know and do God's will, wrestle in anguish over whether they are called to preach. I have always felt more at home behind a pulpit than anywhere on earth.

I can hardly wait from one preaching assignment

to another. Studying and preparing new sermons has never been a chore, but an exciting adventure. For over twenty-five years, preaching and pastoring had not only been my profession and source of income, but my joy, my love, my recreation, my reason for living. I could no more imagine myself without a sermon and a church than I could imagine Lindbergh without a plane and a sky.

You must know how strongly I feel about preaching to know why it was not a simple matter of finding another job. Several friends suggested I try to get a desk job with one of our denominational agencies or institutions. Some were good enough to offer secular jobs they felt I could handle. I knew they were sincerely trying to help, but I kept wondering why no one (outside my immediate family) seemed to understand what preaching really meant to me.

A pulpit committee from a large out-of-state church visited me one Sunday. They were courteous and kind, but quickly and firmly excused themselves, never contacting me again. I could not blame them at all. It must have been a depressing spectacle. I was bloated from my normal 190 pounds to 230 because of the cortisone, was walking laboriously with a cane, sat on a stool through the entire sermon, and preached with a weak, trembling voice. The congregation had shrunk so that the 1,800-seat auditorium was only about one-third filled. No pulpit committee could have been expected to accept that situation with open arms.

By now, it was painfully clear that neither should

I expect my present church to keep me on as pastor. I was honestly doing as much, and sometimes more, than I was physically able to do. With very few exceptions I had continued to conduct all regular worship services. We took no vacations or time off so that the few Sundays out when I was hospitalized were no more than any average pastor misses. The point, however, was that I could do practically nothing else. Weekday activities were limited to absolute emergencies, and I simply did not have the energy to supply the leadership and enthusiasm the church needed.

After skirting the issue for months, and discussing it in vague terms for weeks, Margie and I finally faced the reality of it one day. There was no other logical or ethical option; I must resign and let the church get on with its business.

I visited with our sympathetic area missions secretary and he informed me of what I could expect from our denominational annuity plan for medical retirement. I secured the same kind of information from the Social Security people. I did not have any kind of disability insurance. From all sources, I could expect about $4,000 a year. My present salary was approximately $25,000, so the financial outlook was not the brightest. At an age when most men are getting their biggest promotion and largest increase in salary, I was faced with an 84 percent reduction.

Believing that God knew our needs and would supply them, we began to do our part in preparing for the changeover. Margie got a job with a local insurance company and began work immediately, to help with the mounting bills and fend off an uncertain future. Our daughter began to consider the possibility of dropping out of college to work full time. Our son was only a few weeks away from graduating from college, and he and his wife were both working.

We quietly told a few real estate people that our house was for sale. We had already moved once because of the financial burden of my illness, leaving our beautiful home on the lake. Now it was obvious that we could not even stay in this house. We began to make adjustments and cutbacks, and to try to put aside every penny we could for the rainy days ahead.

We developed an uncanny rapport with those who are faced with sudden retirement and drastically reduced income. It is an emotional experience that is impossible to describe; one has to live through it to understand it. Here we were, in our middle forties, sitting down and trying to figure out how to live on a poverty level income. Our hearts will always be more open and more considerate of those who, through age or disability, come to that traumatic day in their lives. Children who become irritated and impatient with their elderly parents' preoccupation with daily expenses should try to place themselves in that position.

So the plans were made, not in joy, but in faith that God still knew where we were. We decided on a definite day to announce my resignation (retirement?) and a date for it to become effective, all of which would be over within six months.

I had quit running from the dawn. I had accepted the diagnosis. I knew my life as a preacher was over. I went through the preparations mechanically as one must do in preparing for a funeral. Waiting now only for the arrival of the scheduled days, I knew the cry of Job: "When I lie down, I say, when shall I arise, and the night be gone? and I am full of tossings to and fro unto the dawning of the day" (Job 7:4).

THREE

...and stumbled on a morning

When the morning stars sang together,
and all the sons of God shouted
for joy . . .

Job 38:7

FACING A BRIGHT LIGHT

Thou shalt forget thy misery, and remember it as waters that pass away: And thine age shall be clearer than the noonday; thou shalt shine forth, thou shalt be as the morning. And thou shalt be secure, because there is hope (Job 11:16–18).

THE WORMLIKE LARVA does little more than eat, grow large, and molt. It is obsessed with its immediate needs, oblivious to other creatures in its world, and totally unaware of its resplendent destiny.

The larval covering of the ugly caterpillar bears a number of bristles and hairs. It may have wartlike projections or prominent hornlike projections. It has practically no sense of sight; the larva is able to detect only light from darkness.

Growth rates of larvae differ greatly. Some small

simple ones complete larval development in a week, while large, intricate species may take two or more years. Several Arctic varieties spend two winters as larvae.

Then one day the larva stops eating, and after a period of wandering spins a cocoon or enters the ground to pupate. To the outside observer, it appears that the limited, unattractive life of the larva has come to an end. However, on the inside of the lifeless-appearing cocoon, a most marvelous metamorphosis is taking place.

Already present in the newly formed pupa are many partially developed adult structures, and as the distinctively larval structures break down, the adult organs take shape. Wings, which had begun development internally during larval life, break out and complete development externally, remaining soft and capable of swift expansion. Although the adult may be fully formed in a week or two, it may remain many months in the pupal covering.

When the adult finally emerges, it has the exquisite form of a graceful butterfly. The wings of different species show great diversity of size, shape, color, and pattern. But they are all exotically beautiful and breathtakingly magnificent. Even the most pragmatic scientist has difficulty in seeing the relationship of this new life to the old larva, but the secret ways of nature have decreed that the one cannot exist without the other.

AS OUR COMMUNITY INVOLVEMENT continued to shrink, and as we made plans to retire from public leadership, we instinctively drew a closer net around our family circle. We stayed in constant contact with the children, more acutely aware than ever of the importance of milestones in their lives.

I was determined to attend our son's graduation from college although it involved riding in a car for over 400 miles, something I had not been able to do for months. We borrowed my brother's "suburban" so that we could fold down the seats, and let me lie down in the back while Margie drove. It made the trip possible, although uncomfortable.

With several family members helping me up and down the steep bleachers of the coliseum, I was able to attend the commencement exercise at least until Randy received his degree. I could barely shuffle back to the car, experiencing weakness, nausea, and intense pain. I needed to lie down, but I did not think I could climb the stairs again to the second floor of the motel where we had a room. Although we had reservations for another night, Margie and I agreed that we should start for home as quickly as possible.

I had just dropped off to sleep in the back of the suburban when I was jolted awake and slung sideways. Certain that we had had a wreck, I spun around and lunged forward to see if Margie was all right. She was obviously shaken, but firmly bringing the vehicle under control and back into the proper highway lane. A huge buzzard had swept suddenly off a fence at the side of the road, crashing into us with a wrenching impact.

After surveying the damage to the car and to our nerves, we proceeded on our way, but I began immediately developing a strong headache and pain in my neck. It was not unbearable, and I shrugged it off as a reflex from the incident and the accumulation of stress during the whole trip. It was Friday afternoon and I had a wedding to perform Saturday night and two worship services to conduct Sunday. I couldn't let a buzzard and a pain in the neck keep me from these appointments.

Although sleepless nights had become a way of life for me, that night was exceptionally bad. Alternating between pain and muscle spasms, and under frequent medication, I finally fell asleep in the early morning. About five o'clock, my short nap was abruptly interrupted by a violent pain that seemed to tear through my neck. I felt as though someone had struck me with a large board or rod, and I bolted upright, crying for Margie to help me.

We tried everything we knew for several hours to relieve the pain, which only got worse. I remembered reading and hearing from specialists that MS patients could get gradually worse, or they could have a sudden onslaught, leaving them paralyzed. I was sure that this was the beginning of the bitter end I had so long dreaded.

I went to the emergency room at the hospital for multiple injections of powerful pain medication, but nothing helped. I was hospitalized for further treatment and neurological observation. The pain had now spread throughout my shoulder and arm and was so severe that I could not raise my head. I was kept under maximum sedation for several days while a team of doctors tried to determine if this was advanced multiple sclerosis or an entirely different problem.

When a neurosurgeon saw me, he knew almost instantly, from the position in which I was holding my body and the description of pain, that there was the likelihood of a damaged back. He immediately ordered a myelogram, a series of X-rays which outline the shape and size of the spinal cord and reveal any obstruction to the fluid flow. This was the most painful, and yet most fruitful, test to which I had been subjected in two years.

The myelogram showed conclusively that I had extensive damage in the area of three of my seven cervical (neck) vertebrae. There was indication that two of my five lumbar (lower back) vertebrae were also impaired. The suspected damage turned out to be herniated (ruptured) discs.

We learned that the intervertebral discs serve as shock absorbers between adjacent vertebrae. The rubbery central nucleus sometimes degenerates and allows the adjacent vertebrae to rub on each other. The resulting arthritis produces local pain or radiating pain down an extremity. One of my cervical discs had developed a large arthritic ridge such as this. In other cases, the nucleus in the disc escapes through the back wall of the disc, causing spinal cord pressure. This is a protruded or herniated disc, and causes neuritic arm or leg pain, depending upon the location of the spinal lesion. Two of my cervical discs were in an advanced herniated state. The two lumbar discs were not as advanced in deterioration, but were abnormal enough to cause extreme pressure and pain.

Herniated discs in any location may produce pain, limited back movement, muscle spasm, and deformity. The pain may radiate into the arms and legs when nerves are irritated. Prolonged pressure may cause paralysis of an extremity.

As the doctor explained to us briefly and simply what had been happening in my back, we realized he was describing the very symptoms which had led to the diagnosis of multiple sclerosis. Afraid to hope, I hesitantly asked if it were possible that I didn't have MS at all, but only five mutilated discs. He cautiously worded his answer, not wanting to give me false hope, but clearly indicating that he believed that was probably the case.

Other patients, hospital staff, and visitors hardly knew how to respond to the weird joy with which my wife and children excitedly told everyone the "good news" that I had four or five ruptured discs. But we knew the reason for such paradoxical emotions. Herniated discs can be repaired by surgery, and MS cannot. I might have something operable and curable after all. Perhaps my rejection of the diagnosis had been right all along. Obviously, a long ordeal of surgery and hospitalization lay ahead, but hopefully there would be recovery at the end.

Because I was in such immediate pain, the implications of what was happening did not come to me as quickly and as forcibly as they did to my family. It would be several weeks before I could rationally sort things out, but already I was realizing how foolish I had been. I had run from the dawn, afraid to face the truth, and the truth waiting on the horizon of a great new day contained all the hope and joy and life that I had feared was over. I remembered that my primary prayer throughout the ordeal had been that God would enable me to complete the work he had put me here to do. I had begun to visualize, and even plan, ways to fulfill that purpose as an invalid, but I had seen no reason to hope that restoration to full health would ever come. In resignation to the inevitable, I had prayed for divine strength and grace to see me through to the end. In an answer magnificently above and beyond all that I had dared dream, he had turned the end into a new beginning.

I spent practically the entire summer in the hospital. I had three operations, two on my neck and one on the lower back. The cervical discs were repaired and fused with a plug taken from my pelvic bone. The two lumbar discs were completely removed. I wore a rigid body brace for nine weeks to keep the repaired discs perfectly lined up while healing.

Between the second and third operations, a blood clot passed through my heart and into my lung, and I spent an additional eight days in the hospital to avert further dangerous complications. My weakened condition, developed over many months, worked against the healing process, and the heavy dosages of cortisone continued to aggravate the delicate balance of my metabolism.

After each surgery I received immediate relief from some of the symptoms in certain areas. I was concerned as to why I had not been given a myelogram test before, during all the intensive examinations. It was explained to me that my symptoms were so many and so widespread that MS seemed the only logical diagnosis. If I had had only one or two symptoms in a clearly defined area, they would have suspected malfunction in specific areas of the spine. But with five deteriorating discs pressing on large areas of the central nervous system, I was experiencing multiple signals of danger throughout my whole body. It simply never occurred to anyone that I could have that much disc trouble without a serious injury.

It was rather generally agreed that our encounter with the buzzard had triggered the final bursting out of the disc nuclei which had been slowly squeezing on the nerves over many months. Later, Margie found several occasions to tease me about the Lord sending a buzzard to get his preacher back on the track. I protested that if it were so, it seemed terribly unglamorous, for Jonah at least had an impressive whale.

I was, indeed, recovering. The doctor made me throw my cane away and learn to walk independently again. Every day our hopes of reversing the MS diagnosis grew stronger. Prayers were being answered abundantly above what we had expected. Letters and calls of rejoicing and encouragement poured in from friends and churches everywhere. I began to think again of the future in terms of work and ministry instead of retirement and defeat.

The body, however, has its own time schedule, and keeps pace with its own drummer. It will not be rushed by eagerness or impatience. The healing process was slow. The summer dragged by in monotonous sameness. Although I received the finest professional hospital service available anywhere in the country, I was still despondent over my rate, or lack, of progress.

I knew that friends and church members were perplexed over my despondency. I'm sure they felt I should be singing and dancing for joy over the good news. I was thrilled, and as deeply grateful as a man can be. I wept in prayers of gratitude every day. But the plain truth was that my body was thoroughly exhausted. My voice was so weak that I could not speak above a whisper for several weeks. My spinal column and central nervous system had been constantly pressured for two years, and then violently assaulted by three major surgeries only days apart. I was having to be carefully and slowly weaned away from the cortisone. My nerves were completely shot by both the physical and emotional impact of what I had been through. I wept often and uncontrollably. Every day was a major battle for recovery, and I was sometimes my own worst enemy.

I knew now that I would be well again, but I also knew that it would take longer than I and many others would like. I had planned to release the church from their sick pastor in just a few weeks. Could I expect them now to hold on a little longer for full recovery?

The night was over. A new morning had been ushered in with the dawn I had feared to face. But would this new day bring new kinds of burdens and problems? Had I survived the night only to be lost in the day? Or had I gained new insights that would provide reservoirs of strength for the rest of the journey?

AVOIDING UNKNOWN PATHS

Then the Lord answered Job . . . Who is this that darkeneth counsel by words without knowledge? Hast thou commanded the morning since thy days; and caused the dayspring to know his place? (Job 38:1, 2, 12).

THE OLD MAN is saddened as he watches the young child throw a temper tantrum because he can't get his way immediately. The old man does not understand, because he knows the child is old enough to know and do better. He recalls the days of discipline and the years of patience. He remembers learning to wait for nature's unfolding of its seasonable blossoms. He has not forgotten the folly of having too much too soon.

The old man cannot grasp the idea that the child has been programmed for instant gratification. His food is set before him with practically no preparation, bearing the label of "instant" food. With a flip of a switch, his room is flooded with light, or music, or heat, or coolness. He pushes a button and moving pictures flash across his private screen, and live sports events and news events are instantly before his eyes. He touches a small knob at his wrist, and the time is announced in digital numbers. With a hurried scan across the computer keys, complex problems are solved instantly. Even if his parents are not indulgent, granting every whim, he has grown up in a world where expressed demand has instant supply.

He is agitated because he has not yet been able to satisfactorily control the weather and the seasons on command, but he is working on it. There are times when he would like to command the morning to instantly replace his night. He would even like to designate the preferred time and place for the dayspring—the sunrise—to burst forth. And if he hears that there is a supernatural power available through a religious exercise called prayer, he might even try to harness that power to grant some of his desires—instantly.

MY FIRST SUNDAY back in the pulpit was a momentous occasion for me, and I think also for the patient, rejoicing church. An extra large crowd was on hand to welcome me with a standing ovation. My voice trembled from both physical weakness and emotional overspill.

I preached that morning on the experience of

Jonah (Margie asked me later why I had omitted the comparison between the buzzard and the whale). My emphasis was on the second chance Jonah was given to continue his ministry (Jonah 3:1, 2). Naturally, I made the obvious application to myself and the church, as we had been given a second chance for service together.

In the course of my remarks, I thanked the church for all they had done. Although I had continued to write my gratitude in the weekly column of the church paper, I was glad to be able to stand before them and tell them in person how much their prayers and support had meant to us. I also expressed appreciation for other churches and friends, for the excellent medical staff, and the superb hospital service I had received. Most of all I thanked God.

During the ensuing days, many people expressed delight over the "miraculous" healing which God had given me. However, there were some (locally and in distant cities) who were disappointed that I had not used the word "miracle" in my testimony. There are many believers who need to have their faith affirmed or validated by supernatural miracles. It is almost an assault on their spiritual security for someone to forfeit the golden opportunity I had to promote the Christian religion with a sensational healing story. Their faith simply has to have daily strengthening: they are certainly not malicious in their expressions of disappointment.

On the other hand, there are those who are adamant about the matter and strong in their convictions about miraculous faith healing. Such pure conviction is to be admired, if it is accompanied by the spirit of Christian love. I have been quite frankly confused about the motives of some who had insisted that I submit to their faith healing techniques. After I was healed through normal medical procedures, they never offered a word of rejoicing or thanksgiving. How could they drop out of my life so quickly and completely with never another word, if they had been as burdened and concerned for my suffering as they had said so often? I am still trying to accept the fact that there are some Christians who demand that your commitment, and even God's acts, conform to their idea of religion.

There are, however, many fine Christians in every community who are sincerely wanting to know when to expect and how to recognize a bona fide miracle. I have been asked many questions such as: "You have really experienced a miracle, haven't you?" or "Wouldn't you call your healing a modern day miracle?" I have understood all such comments as wanting to give God the glory for answered prayer, and have agreed that he has done a marvelous work in my life. I have certainly not wanted to offend anyone's faith on technical wording. Yet there is for me personally a vital principle of theological integrity involved in speaking of miracles.

I realize that it may just be a matter of working with certain definitions. For those who define a miracle as any answer to prayer, there are a great many miracles in my story and in yours. For those who say a miracle is anything which God does that man cannot do, the whole earth is bursting with the creative miracles of God. The biblical record of miracles, however, does not convey either of these concepts.

The proper theological definition of a miracle, based on the biblical witness, is that it is an event in this world of ours, not grounded on the continuity of other events in this world; nor is it to be understood in terms of it. It is a unique sign set up immediately by God, and should be understood as such. *A miracle is by definition an exception.* A new and different event is fed into the natural pattern of things when a miracle occurs. It is obvious to rational men that something supernatural has occurred.

I believe that God, in his sovereign power over his universe, not only can but has performed miracles. I believe the biblical record of miracles to be the accurate historical account of God's supernatural intervention. I believe that God is still able to perform miracles today if he deems them necessary for signs or revelations. I do not deny the historicity or present possibility of miracles. But I do not think that every beautiful event, or even every creative act of God fits the definition of a miracle.

For instance, there is a lovely song which says, "I believe in miracles. . . . I've seen the lily push its way up through the stubborn sod." The growth of the lily is a beautiful, marvelous expression of God's order of the universe. But it is not a miracle; it is, in fact, just the reverse. A miracle is something which happens contrary to the ordinary laws of nature. A flower's growth is in accordance with natural laws, God's laws.

The sunrise and sunset are marvelous and beautiful scenes every day, but they are not miracles. The birth of a child is a wondrous, marvelous occurrence in nature, but it is not a miracle. If we call every lovely and happy event a miracle, then we will eliminate the very possibility of miracles, for miracles are not ordinary, but extraordinary acts of God. Our problem is that we have such a difficult time conceding that an ordinary act can be just as much the work of God as the extraordinary. The solution to our problem is to believe in a God great enough and wise enough to act in the ordinary or extraordinary way as he sees best.

I believe that God works in many ways, his will to accomplish and his wonders to perform. Some of these ways are miraculous and very limited in number. Others are marvelous and happen innumerable times every day. Miraculous and marvelous are two different things.

In my recent illness and healing, I believe God was at work, marvelously but not miraculously. It was not miraculous (the introduction of a new element into the physical world) when my discs ruptured and were repaired by surgery and modern medicine. Well-meaning friends tried to get me to testify that God miraculously healed me from MS. But the truth is that I never did have MS, only a very messed up back. My healing was not miraculous, but it certainly was marvelous.

It was marvelous that we were in the right place at the right time to receive the proper treatment, and I believe God was in that. It was marvelous that our financial needs were met in an unexpected way, and I believe God led in that. It was marvelous that our family and our work and our attitude and our church were all sustained through those many months, and I believe God was in all of that. It was marvelous that each need was met as it arose, that wisdom was given when decisions had to be made, that people and events all synchronized in a plan that, now, in retrospect, was clearly of God's doing.

But in all this doing of marvelous things, we saw the Lord working through natural processes, through his church, through people who made themselves available by training and resources. Yes, a thousand times yes, God was working, and by doing so was answering many prayers. But we must not give instructions to God as to *how* he will answer prayers, and we must not insist on naming everything he does a miracle. What we must do is to believe implicitly in *him*, not the process. We must be committed to his will, not to magical powers.

Rejoice with me that God has done a marvelous thing in my body and life. Join me in prayer for others who need to receive and recognize his marvelous work in countless ways. Then let us leave divine miracles in the hands of God to be performed and revealed in his wisdom.

GEARING DOWN FOR STEEP HILLS

Surely it is meet to be said unto God, I have borne chastisement, I will not offend anymore (Job 34:31).

IT WAS OVER. The long dreadful struggle had left him exhausted, but still alive. He had wrestled the angel of God and survived. His name was changed from Jacob to Israel. He had finally come into the circle of God's plan.

His clothes were soaked from the perspiration of the battle exertion. His chest heaved up and down as he strained to refill his lungs with air. His mind flashed back across the years that had culminated in this night of agony and ecstasy.

He remembered with gratitude his godly heritage which he ill deserved; the heavenly visions and divine promises which had guided him; the prosperity of vocation and the happiness of home.

He recalled with regret his selfishness and greed; his schemes to trick his father and cheat his brother; his cunning plots against his uncle; his constant running from the Voice that would not stop calling him.

But it was over now. The running, the selfishness, the wasted talents were all yielded. He knew it would be different now. He was ready to serve this God who had wrestled him face to face.

He stood, ready to walk into a new day. But as he stepped forward, he stumbled and fell, clutching his thigh that had been thrown out of joint. He pulled himself erect again, realizing he would never be the same man again; but knowing that he had to give his God what was left, he limped into the sunrise.

THE DOCTORS had cautioned me that I was returning to the pulpit about two months sooner than I should, but they understood my eagerness to pick up my life again, a life that I had thought was all but over only a few weeks earlier. I paid for my eagerness with minor relapses and long spells of weakness.

The church had endured not only the summer of my surgeries, but the long months of anxiety and uncertainty prior to them. I felt that they needed assurance that all was well, that they had a healthy pastor again. Previously I had worn a happy mask to keep them from knowing how rapidly I was going downhill. Now, I put the same mask back on to keep them from knowing how steep that hill was that I was trying to climb again.

A man can talk about himself too much, especially if he is in the pulpit to proclaim Christ. But I am learning that a man can also talk about himself too little. People need to know certain things about their leaders, especially those things that will help them to know what is needed and expected from them. We cannot always assume that people automatically know our situation and our related needs. Sometimes they should be, and want to be, told plainly what is going on.

Suffering is so acute to the person undergoing the pain that he is apt to feel that the whole world is centered around his personal agony. When this happens, he either thinks that everyone knows his needs, or he doesn't want anyone to know how desperate he feels. Both extremes result in the same stoical silence, keeping helpful information locked away.

Relatively speaking, my recovery from three surgeries for multiple disc problems was incredibly successful. Many people who have had surgery on just one disc have not done as well as I. Except for the normal effects of this kind of surgery, most of my problems have either decreased or disappeared altogether. I will never be able to lift anything very heavy (but I never did want to anyway). Long trips on rough roads are especially hard because of the removal of the cushion which the lower discs had provided. I never expect to ride horses or go water skiing again, but two years ago I hadn't expected to walk again. Otherwise, I am working average schedules and living a normal life.

But it didn't happen as easily as it sounds, and the effects of the long recovery period went beyond the obviously physical. I had usually followed the pattern of society's thinking that an illness is over and done with when a person goes home from the hospital. I have learned that the most frustrating part of the episode may be just beginning.

There are the frightening relapses, the recurring weak spells, and the deep depressions. There are the ever-present fears that the surgery was not successful, that you're taking the wrong medicine, that you're going to hurt yourself again. There is worry over the bills piling up, worry over time passing you by, and worry over whether you will really be able to go back to work.

Worst of all, there are the long days of loneliness. The patient usually gets most of his visits, calls, and mail when he is hospitalized, and so sick he can't even acknowledge the thought. When he has time to visit and needs people to talk to, they have gone on their way, thinking he is well now. We have always done it this way and are not likely to change, but reminders may help us to be more tolerant and thoughtful.

Some of life's most important decisions come when we are least able to handle them. Only a few weeks out of the hospital, I received an invitation from our denominational leaders to become the editor of a new series of curriculum materials. I was still so weak that I did not feel that I could even make the flight back east for the interview. Even though they gave me an extension on the deadline to decide, I knew I had to decline. I was beginning to doubt if I would ever be strong enough for such enterprises again.

In the slowly dragging months of mending, I felt that I was ineffective at both pastoral leadership and at body rebuilding. Ironically, I began to have more self-pity than I did when I thought I had MS. I realized that an incurable disease has to finally be accepted with the realization that no one is immune, but now that I knew I did not have an incurable disease, I could not understand this waste of time. My logic was that if God had brought me through, he must have something more for me to do and I was eager to get to it.

About this time, another local pastor who had been a confirmed MS patient for fifteen years was forced to go into medical retirement. Also, another friend who had been medically retired from the Air Force chaplaincy because of MS became much worse and almost completely bedfast. I was suddenly ashamed of my self-pity. I was fretting over a slow recovery, and there were brave men and women all around me who would never recover at all.

I thought much of those soldiers of suffering during those days, and in many days to follow. Most people are momentarily compassionate when they see someone crippled or paralyzed or in some other way disabled, and they may murmur in their grateful hearts, "There, but for the grace of God, go I." They think little, if any, beyond the moment of encounter, and go on their healthy way. They do not realize that, as bad as it looks, what they are seeing of the victim's condition in public is probably the best part of his existence. Beyond the public eye, there is the nonstop pain or never-improving disability. There are personal inconveniences, social embarrassments, family problems, complicated decisions, financial pressures, medication adjustments, hospital confinements, and disappointed hopes.

Frustrations about whether you are receiving the best medical advice and treatment constantly hover around, with many people suggesting a better hospital or a better doctor. My experience with this common reaction did not end with the lifting of the MS scare.

In fact, numerous people suggested that I should even sue the doctors who had incorrectly diagnosed my condition, causing additional expenses, longer suffering, and great anxiety. I could not, however, feel that this was a proper action. In the first place, I knew that every doctor and medical technician had been conscientious and sincere. Having to work with an unusual set of symptoms, they seemed to follow a natural course. I had no desire to punish anyone; I had seen my fill of people hurting. With my new lease on life I felt I was the richest man on earth, and making money off someone's mistake was a distasteful thought. Besides, I was eager to put all this behind me and get on with a productive life of work and service.

Those who have not shared the night of the disabled perhaps do not understand the despondency over not being able to work. Some disabled have no pain and plenty of money, and observers may wonder why they are so depressed, but no normal person wants to be totally dependent. Everyone wants the opportunity to exercise his abilities, supply his own needs, and try for his dream. Now, when I see a disabled person, my first thought is not about his or her pain or financial needs, for I know these can usually be overcome some way. I wonder what dreams have been shattered, what plans had to be abandoned, what relationships were destroyed, and what they are now doing to compensate.

During recuperation, I naturally thought much about the meaning of life in general, and the purpose of my life in particular. Soon after my successful surgeries, I told a prominent minister friend that I felt like Lazarus, the man Jesus had raised from the dead, and that God had given me a beautiful second chance at life. I asked my friend if he knew what Lazarus did with the rest of his life, and he said, "No, I don't, but I'll bet he laughed a lot."

I knew the feeling. It seems that I was on the verge of crying or laughing all the time. I knew, however, that God wanted more from me than laughter. I felt that the most adequate way to express my gratitude would be to discover exactly what God wanted me to do with my life and give myself to that single-minded purpose with all my heart.

By now, I was becoming realistic about some things I could never do well again, if at all. Some of these things related to my pastoral services, and I had to be exceptionally candid with myself in evaluating the importance of what I could and could not do. In the process of evaluation, I also discovered that I had changed spiritually and philosophically, as well as physically. This was a hard fact to admit or understand, for I had always felt that beliefs and convictions should remain intact regardless of one's physical circumstances.

I knew now, for instance, that my whole concept of success had changed, and that I simply did not have, anymore, that lifelong ambition to be the best preacher in the country. It wasn't a matter of humility winning over pride, or praying myself into a submissive attitude. I just simply didn't have that particular drive or dream anymore.

The brevity of life and the certainty of death had become big factors in all my thinking. I thought constantly of how little time was left. I had thought it was all over; now I had another chance; but now I also knew that someday, somewhere it truly would be over. What can I, what *must* I do before then? I was obsessed to find the answer, and even if I had to limp into the sunrise like Jacob, I was ready.

TAKING A NEW TURN

Thou shalt call, and I will answer thee: thou wilt have a desire to the work of thine hands (Job 14:15).

THE THOROUGHBRED ran his last race with the same gusto as his previous contests. He did not know, of course, that it was his last race. He was only a horse, and knew nothing of the plans of his owners, the negotiations over his future, and the speculations of the public.

He only knew that he was born to run, trained to run, and loved to run. He did not understand the crowds and the noise, the hoping and the betting, the trophies and the prize money. But he did understand, and respond to, the feel of the track, the breath of his nearest rival, and the prodding of his rider.

His natural reflexes and trained responses had to

adjust to his new world. The long days in the pasture were strange to him, and he paced the fences, impatient to be off and running again.

Gradually, he began to adopt his new role of setting the pace for younger colts, being the example for trainers' instructions, and producing a new generation of thoroughbreds.

He often dreamed of returning to the track, but something surged up inside him, demanding his best for this day and this work.

DURING MY LONG CONVALESCENCE, I had reopened the work on my doctoral dissertation. I had abandoned it because I was physically unable to do the work and I could not see any purpose for it. Now it became a symbol of a new beginning and some kind of future after all.

My alma mater had granted me an honorary doctorate in the midst of my severest illness, and I was humbly grateful. But the earned doctorate, with its academic substance and scholarly training, was still something I felt I personally needed. My vocational intentions had not changed, but I felt a strong providential guidance back to the degree project.

I began writing on the dissertation again while I was still wearing the body brace, and continued for several months, until I completed all the requirements and was awarded the Ph.D. degree the next spring. As I stood in line waiting to cross the stage to receive my diploma, a young man in a wheelchair was rolled across directly in front of me. Totally paralyzed, he was concluding a monumental achievement, and received a well-deserved thundering applause. With tears in my eyes, I remembered too vividly that only one year ago I had been shopping for wheelchairs and never dreamed that I would walk across this stage.

The following fall I was asked to teach two courses as an emergency substitute at my alma mater, the university across the street from our church. The arrangement seemed ideal and offered me an opportunity to reestablish relationships with the university which I had neglected during my illness. I felt that it was a God-given opportunity for the church to recruit more students and increase its role as a university church.

The experience on campus was more satisfying than I had ever anticipated. The interchange with stimulating young minds stirred me intellectually and spiritually. The ease and enthusiasm with which I performed in this new role demanded that I honestly reconsider my determination to remain a full-time pastor.

During this same period of time I was approached by several publishers and asked to write articles, Sunday school commentaries, devotional books, and some longer projects. While I had been involved for many years in occasional writing, I was now being crowded to think about a more serious ministry of writing. The whole issue of spiritual gifts became a big item in my personal Bible study as I sought to understand what God wanted from me.

The basic passages which deal with the spiritual

gifts Christians receive for service are Romans 12:4–8; 1 Corinthians 12:4–31; and Ephesians 4:7, 11–13. In these references, it is clear that (1) all gifts are from God and not man; that (2) God allots these gifts according to his own sovereign will, as he deems best; that (3) all gifts, regardless of how they are seen by the world, are of equal importance in the divine scheme; and that (4) the gifts are for the explicit purpose to serve and complement the whole church, not for personal pleasure or glory.

Having always had such an unquestionable call to preach, I had assumed this meant as a full-time pastor, evangelist, or missionary. While I admired the teaching profession, I never thought of myself in that capacity. Now I found that if I were to be honest about being open to any call of God, it had to include this possibility also.

As I tried to list my gifts and personal preference of vocations in an order of priorities, I found myself repeating the order of preaching, teaching, and writing. As I prayed earnestly to know God's will over a period of several months, I kept sensing the insistent message from God that if I would be willing to trust him, he would make it possible for me to utilize all three of the gifts.

I did not want to leave the pastorate. I was afraid that yielding to whatever God revealed would include that possibility. Consequently, I turned down the invitation to teach part-time again the next semester, and gave myself completely to the pastoral ministries. I was determined to prove this was where I belonged. God would not reward my stubbornness with his blessings, and I realized he was still waiting for me to let him take control.

Then I recalled how I had run from the dawn during my physical illness, afraid to learn the truth, and how incredibly marvelous the truth turned out to be, ushering in the brightest morning of my life. If God could do that so beautifully with my physical needs, couldn't he also have unexpected blessings waiting in my vocational commitment? As sincerely as I knew how, I told God I was totally surrendered to being and doing whatever he desired.

Almost immediately upon my yielding, I was asked to teach full-time at the university. It would naturally seem the obvious answer to my prayer, but I was afraid because it was too obvious and too simple. I had expected something more unusual or unknown to appear on the horizon. Besides, it is one thing to say you will surrender, and quite another when you are faced with the reality and terms of that surrender. I asked for additional time to decide, to wait for other options to develop, and to ask myself if I could really do it.

Could I live happily and productively out of the pastorate? How vital was the close relationship of pastor and people to me? Would I be able to hold up under the criticism of "leaving the ministry"? Could I do the job and make a permanent place for myself in a new world? Was my personality and motivation dependent on the spotlight that shines on the pastor?

Even if I could handle all of these aspects of the move myself, was it fair to ask Margie to share this change? I knew she loved the pastorate, delighted in her Sunday school class, and served effectively in every relationship. But I also knew that she had never complained about our moves, always trusted me to follow God's will, and would move agreeably wherever I felt he was leading. When she was only twenty-five years old, Margie had survived an advanced malignancy, and the memory of her faith and courage during those dark days had inspired me in my own recent illness. She had sustained me in every step of the long journey we had traveled together, and I knew she still would.

Together we prayed, and hurt, and cried, and waited, and prayed again. Together we knew when the time had come, and together we felt exactly the same about the decision.

The resignation was one of the hardest ever, because I was not only resigning from a local church, but from the pastorate, after twenty-eight joy-filled years. Yet I told the church that I was not leaving the ministry or forsaking the mission of the church; I believed God was leading me to serve churches with greater depth than ever by preparing their future leaders.

My first teaching assignments proved these words to be accurate, almost prophetic. I was to teach biblical studies, church history, sermon preparation, the work of the pastor, and direct the field guidance program for ministerial students. How could I ever be more creatively involved in the ministry of the church? In addition, invitations to speak in area churches started coming immediately, reassuring me that I would have all the pulpit work I would ever want.

The church accepted our going graciously, and assured us of their prayer support in our new venture. They regrouped and began planning for future ministries. My decision proved to be as right and healthy for the church as it was for me.

Our apprehensions changed to confidence, and our expectations blossomed into excitement. We approached our new ministry with joy, knowing now that God had been preparing me for this all along. Supportive affirmations came from so many quarters that any previous worries about criticism now seemed foolish. An all-sufficient Father indicated in numerous ways that he could and would provide for his children if they would trust and obey him.

My days are now crammed with assignments and appointments and deadlines, but there is no panic or confusion because everything seems purposefully related to my threefold ministry of preaching, teaching, and writing. There is a peace and a joy that opens and closes every day.

There are also shadows that linger, memories that will not fade, and nightmares that have a hard time dying. But they are being replaced brightly and firmly by two permanent impressions. First, there is the indescribable awareness of a fresh new air about everything. Then, there is the tenacious companionship of suffering that will always reserve a part of my heart for the incurably ill and their families.

For a brief time I shared their long journey of despair. For some reason I have yet to discover, I was given the chance to step back into the sunlight. I can never completely let go of those courageous hearts who will live out their days in the shadows, but have drunk deeper of life's meaning than most of us in perfect health ever shall.

I salute them and their loved ones, and all our true friends in Christ who have kept me close to the God "who giveth songs in the night" (Job 35:10) and who, in his own way and his own time, "setteth an end to darkness" (Job 28:3).